Former NFL Veteran Robert Tate

Reveals How He made it from Little League to the NFL

Overcoming A Secret Battle With Dyslexia

10. Brett

By: Robert Tate

Robert Tate

Robert Tate

This Book is Dedicated

To my father, Robert Lee Tate, Sr. Even though your life was cut short too soon, I will always hold you in my heart. It brings a smile to my face whenever I think about the special father-son bond we shared when I was growing up. You introduced me to sports at a very young age and I loved playing the game ever since, especially basketball. I know you have been smiling down upon me throughout my football career.

I wish you could have met your grandchildren: Shekia, Malachi, Arriana and Robert III. They are great children and are growing up so fast. Your oldest granddaughter Shekia will be graduating high school this year. You would have been so proud of them all. But, I know you are looking down and smiling upon all things that your grandchildren do.

I love you dad.

Robert Tate

Acknowledgements

To my mother Michele Tate Washington:
Thank you for standing by me and for always trusting and believing in me. You are the wind beneath my wings. You have always been there for me and your love has made a difference in my life. You have been the inspiration for all my accomplishments and I am so thankful to have you as my mother. You have helped me to become the man I am today. I love you mom.

To my step-father Thomas Washington:
Thank you for always believing in me and for making my mom smile. I see you as a man of principle who stands up for what he believes in. I see you as a man I admire more than words can say and I'm very happy and proud to have you as my step-dad. I love you Thomas.

Robert Tate

Acknowledgments (continued)

To former Mayor Stephen R. Reed: Thank you so much for your support over the years. I was humbled by being the recipient of the "Mayor's Award for Distinguished Public Service" in 2001 and I try to live up to that honor each day. Your support and belief in me has always been respected.

To Joshua Flatt: I have to give kudos to you for doing an amazing job in guiding me in the structure and syntax of this book project. Thank you so much for your guidance during the writing of this book.

To everyone who assisted me in anyway as I broke through barriers to get the education I deserved and to achieve the success I have achieved; I want you to know I could not have made it as far as I did without your assistance. Thank you so much!

Robert Tate

CONTENTS

PART FOUR

PART FIVE

Robert Tate

Foreword

Former Mayor Stephen R. Reed
City of Harrisburg

Robert Tate has distinguished himself in a manner in which all young people should aspire, both while he graced the halls of Harrisburg High until his graduation in 1992 and most certainly in the time since.

Robert Tate's legacy sends a powerful message to every young person in this city and nation – a message that each person can do whatever he or she sets one's mind and heart to achieving and that, to be successful, each person should set personal goals and be willing to work hard to meet them.

Equally important is the very nature of this respected young man, who is motivated by the higher values and ideals of civic duty and personal responsibility. Robert gives back to his community and those in need, and he serves as a true role model for all citizens to admire and emulate.

Robert Tate

Introduction by Robert Tate

I am going to take you through my journey from the Little League to the NFL. As you will see during my journey, I went through my share of trials and tribulations. The roads got a little bumpy and curvy at times, but I still kept on going. There were times when I just wanted to throw in the towel and be done with it all. But with the love, support and guidance of my mom, and my own determination, I was able to pull myself together and get back on track.

Life is made up of memorable moments. Some are good, some not so good. I am going to share these memories with you, the good, the bad and the ugly. I have opened up a part of my life that I have never shared before. During the writing of this book, I have re-visited places that have been very painful for me. But I needed to do it in order to overcome it.

This is the story of how I got to where I am today and some of the great lessons I've learned along the way. For all you football fans out there, there is plenty of pigskin in the pages that follow; never before written details of my life. I will tell you how I made it from Little League to the NFL and why I chose football over basketball. Here is my story . . .

Robert Tate

PART ONE

Robert Tate

CHAPTER 1

The NFL Draft

On draft day, Saturday, April 19, 1997, when I was 25-years-old, my family and I were all sitting around at home, in uptown Harrisburg, PA watching the NFL Draft on TV and . . . waiting. There were quite a few people in our house on draft day: my mom, my step-dad Thomas, my little brother and my two little sisters, several aunts and uncles (my mom's sisters and brothers), some cousins, some friends of mine and some family friends. You could feel the excitement in the air. The NFL draft was taking place live at the Theater in New York at Madison Square Garden.

While we were all glued to the TV watching the draft that began at 11:00 that morning, my mom was busy in the kitchen preparing a "Draft Day" meal of steak, fried chicken, macaroni and cheese, potato salad, collard greens, rice, yams, and cornbread for everyone to eat. We had a TV on in the living room, dining room and even a small eight-inch TV in the kitchen. People were gathered in

21

every room in the house, talking and eating and constantly looking at one of the TVs. Everyone was excited that I was about to be drafted in the NFL Draft.

My agent, Ron Delduca, had informed me the week prior to the draft that he heard I did a great job in the NFL Combines and that he was told by prominent draft analysts that I should be drafted somewhere between the third and fourth rounds. There was also a big news story in our local Patriot News newspaper saying where I would most likely be drafted in the NFL. So everyone was expecting something good for me. My family was all psyched up as they were waiting for my name to be called. Then the third round came and went and my name still had not been called. As the draft entered the late rounds, I was beginning to get a little worried but I tried not to show it. Then the fourth round came and went without my name being called. Family and friends kept calling my house asking if I had been drafted yet. I just wanted this to be over with because I hated just waiting around. Then my agent called me and said he was talking to some NFL teams and for me to try to be patient.

But to my disappointment, at 7:00pm Day 1 of the draft came to an end. The first day of the draft had come and gone without me being drafted. I felt like someone had just sucker-punched me in the gut. I felt terrible. Everyone began to leave. As they were leaving, they said I would have better luck tomorrow. My mom and her friend Mae were clearing up the dishes when my mom noticed how down my mood was and she stopped what she was doing and said "Pint, let me talk to you a minute." We sat on the couch and she said, "You know how good you are, and those NFL coaches know too. Now you may not have been selected in the draft today, but keep your head up, because I have a good feeling that things are going to be a lot different for you tomorrow. So keep the faith, keep your head held high and stop worrying so much because everything is going to be alright."

I said okay. I hung out with my friends for a little while that night, then I called it an early night. I fell asleep wondering if I would be drafted the next day.

On the second day of the draft, I woke up at about 7:00 a.m. and began to pace the floors; I did not get much sleep because I was so anxious about the draft. My mom told me to relax and stop being so jumpy. Thomas and I sat at the kitchen table while my mom fixed some grits, fried potatoes, bacon, eggs and toast. I did not have much of an appetite but I ate a little anyway. My little brother and sisters were still asleep. Thomas and I talked about the draft a little bit but he could tell my heart wasn't in it. So he changed the subject. I was still a little nervous about the draft so I told my mom and Thomas that I was going to drive to Baltimore to take to my mind of the draft for a little while. I left home at about 9:00am.

My mom said she was going to church at our church home, Macedonia Missionary

Baptist Church, that morning which was only two blocks up the street from our house. Thomas said he would stay home to watch the draft when it came on at 11:00 that morning. He said he would call my mom at the church if my name was called while she was still there. I asked my mom or Thomas to call me on my cell phone if my name was called before I returned home. I only drove to Baltimore and turned around and drove right back home. As I was driving back, I began to think about all the crappy things that had happened to me over the years. I remembered as a teenager, losing my father when I needed him the most; I remembered in high school being chosen but not being able to play in the McDonald's All-American High School Basketball Game and I remembered graduating but not being able to get a scholarship to a Division 1 college because I failed my SAT. So I thought, "What makes me think that I would be chosen for the NFL?" At that point, I did not think it was even possible. I drove home prepared to accept the fact that I would not be drafted in the 1997 NFL Draft. Of course I kept these thoughts to myself.

The draft began at 11:00 a.m. My mom returned home from church at about 12:00 p.m. and I came home shortly afterwards. My aunts, uncles and a few friends returned to my house to finish watching the draft. The phone rang a few times but after that, my mom asked people not to call anymore because I was expecting a phone call from the NFL Draft. (I thought to myself – am I?) We were now in the 6th round of the draft, nothing yet. Unlike the lively mood yesterday, today the mood was a little reserved as we continued to watch the draft. We were all making small talk and commenting on the picks that were being selected, when the phone rang again. Mom answered and after a few words, she smiled and said it was for me. I took the phone and it was Bill Parcells, Head Coach of the New York Jets! He told me if I was still available, they were going to select me with their next pick. So he asked me to be near the phone. I was so relieved to finally get this call and I felt great! I thanked him for calling and said I would be near the phone. Everyone began congratulating me like I had already been selected.

I quickly let them know that I did not hear those words yet. A few minutes after coach Parcells' called, my agent called me. He said that he had been talking to a couple of different teams and for me to stay near the telephone. Five minutes later the phone rang again, I answered it on the second ring and it was Dennis Green, Head Coach of the Minnesota Vikings! He said, "Robert, you know, we're going to get you."

As he was speaking I looked at the television on ESPN2 and there was my name flashing, "Round 6, 183rd Overall Pick, Minnesota Vikings select Robert Tate, Wide Receiver, Drafted from the University of Cincinnati." I could hardly believe what I was hearing and seeing. The phone call with Coach Green was very brief, he said he would call me back later with further information. All I had the chance to say to Coach Green was, "I won't let you down." I could not believe that I was talking to Dennis Green, Head Coach of the Minnesota Vikings and now here I was, selected to play for them. I was the 19th pick in the 6th round of the draft. I wanted somebody to pinch me to make sure I wasn't dreaming. All I could do was look up and say thank God!

My family went crazy! Everyone was shouting their congratulations to me! My mom and Thomas immediately hung a pre-printed banner across our front porch that said Robert Tate was drafted by the Minnesota Vikings! Of course they had to write Vikings in BIG BLACK LETTERS to make it more noticeable. People who were driving down the street began blowing their horns when they saw the banner. Coach Dennis Green called me again about an hour later, I answered the phone again and he said the Viking organization will fly me from Harrisburg International Airport to Minnesota the next morning to meet him and other members of the Vikings' organization. My mom and Thomas drove me to the airport the next morning. When we got to the airport, they both gave me a big hug and wished me well. My mom had tears in her eyes as she gave me one final hug and kiss before I got on the airplane. I asked her what was wrong and she said they were tears of happiness for me. I said, "I love you mom."

When I arrived in Minnesota, a Viking team executive was waiting for me in the airport. After I got my luggage, he escorted me in a black limousine to the Viking Headquarters where I met Coach Dennis Green, owner Red McCombs and the Viking front office staff. I attended a mini camp along with the other draft picks where we spent time working out, lifting weights, running routes, and getting to know one another.

I returned home after two weeks of working out and lifting weights in Minnesota.

I then spent two days in suburban Chicago at an NFL-sponsored symposium for rookies that covered topics like drugs, alcohol, sex, financial management and life after football.

It was now official; I had a job as a football player for the National Football League! I was represented by my agent in my contract negotiations. When all the dust had cleared, I received a $40,000 signing bonus (not bad for a 6th round draft pick) and I signed a three-year six-figure contract with the Minnesota Vikings!

Albeit this was a huge step for me, it was only the first step. Now that the preliminaries were out of the way, I had my sights set on one major thing, and that was making the team. That process began early the next month. The draft was ancient history. The contract had been signed and mini-camp was over. Now it was time to put the pads on.

I was set and I was signed and I had my signing bonus. All I needed to do now was make the Viking roster.

PART TWO

Robert Tate

CHAPTER 2

My Childhood

I was born on October 19, 1972 in the city of Harrisburg, PA. I was the first child of Michele Lee Burnett and Robert Lee Tate, Sr. who were teenage parents when I was born.

I had a happy childhood growing up. My young life and teenage life were filled with friends and sports. Even though I grew up as an only child, I cannot ever remember feeling lonely. Since my dad came from a large family of ten and my mom came from a large family, I had a lot of cousins to play with. I do remember wishing I had a brother, but that thought did not consume me because I had a lot of cousins around my age and I had a lot friends. I went from one sport to the next: baseball, basketball and football. My parents always seemed to take the time to show up at many of my games, which always meant a lot to me. Even then, I knew they were proud of me.

My mom told me that when I was born, I was so tiny that I could be held in one hand. My great-aunt, Juanita Burke, started calling me Pint because I was so small. Even when I

31

got older and outgrew the name, somehow the name Pint stuck. Today, all my family and friends in Harrisburg still call me Pint. Everyone else calls me either Robert or Tate.

Everyone called my dad by his middle name of Lee. My dad taught me how to play basketball and how to throw a football and I really enjoyed it! As time went on, I couldn't wait until I was able to play football on a real football team and basketball on a real basketball team.

My dad's favorite football team was the Dallas Cowboys. On many Sundays you could find him and his buddies glued to the TV drinking wine and watching the Dallas Cowboys. His favorite basketball team was the LA Lakers. He lived and breathed the Lakers.

My Parents Wedding Day

On July 19, 1980, my mom and dad got married. I was seven-years-old at the time. The wedding ceremony took place at Macedonia Missionary Baptist Church. It was a big wedding and I was in it as the ring-bearer. I remember my mom looking very pretty in her white wedding gown. I had on a black tuxedo with tails, just like my dad wore. My grandpop had on a black tuxedo too but he didn't have the tails. He gave my mom away. My mom and dad had a nice wedding.

After the wedding, I got to ride with my mom and dad in the shiny black limousine on our way to their wedding reception. The wedding party followed us in their cars that were decorated with streamers and beeping their horns in acknowledgement that my mom and dad had just gotten married.

Little League Football

I started playing little league football when I was seven years old. My first football game was on the Peewee football team for the East Shore Royals. I was a defensive back. Even at that young age, my parents must have seen some potential in me because my dad used to always say, "My boy has got natural talent and he is going to go far in life, and son, I am going to help you to make it anyway that I can." My dad was an all-star point guard for the William Penn Tigers when he was in high school and he always talked to me about the game. He said he had missed his opportunity for success with sports because he dropped out of high school. But he always said, "Son, I want you to be a greater success than I ever was and sports can bring you that success." He said, "I see raw talent in you as an athlete and it is going to take you far in life; just make sure you stay in school and get your education, the sports will take care of itself because you have a natural talent for the game."

Every year I was involved in football: first for the Little League Peewees, then the Ponies, Midgets, junior high, high school, prep school, college and the NFL. In between, I played baseball and basketball. My mom said I was ready to play football even before I was allowed to play football.

When I was ten-years-old, I changed leagues and started playing for the Packers in the Uptown League as a Little League Pony.

My dad bought me an electric football game for my 11th birthday and I used to play with it all the time. It was so much fun playing this game. I used to play my electric football game by myself, with my friends and with my dad. Afterwards, my dad and I would shoot the breeze watching football on TV. My dad used to always talk to me about basketball and football and I would remember all the teams and most of the players that he would talk about.

Diagnosed with Dyslexia

As I was enjoying playing football and getting better everyday, I was beginning to struggle in school. Actually, I had been struggling with my school work since first grade. I didn't understand why I couldn't learn my basic ABCs that all the other kids could recite by heart. That's when I first started memorizing my school work. My teachers said I was not focusing. They said I would probably never be able to focus. No matter how hard I tried, I continued to struggle with my school work. When I was in the 5th grade, I was diagnosed as having dyslexia. My parents now understood why I was having so much trouble with my school work and they were both relieved and concerned with this diagnosis. Since there is no cure for dyslexia, I knew that I would always have to work harder in school than my peers if I wanted to keep up.

Dyslexia affects a part of the brain that causes a person to have great difficulty in reading, comprehension, spelling and penmanship. Contrary to the stereotype of dyslexia, it is not an intellectual disability. dyslexia is diagnosed in children in all levels of intelligence: average, above average, highly intelligent and gifted. Usually, what a dyslexic person lacks in academic skills, he/she excels in other areas, such as music, art, sports, etc. In my internet research of dyslexia, I discovered there are many famous people who have dyslexia; one of them is Magic Johnson. He is a 6' 9" former NBA basketball star who played for the Los Angeles Lakers during the 1980s and early 1990s and won several NBA National Championship titles.

When I was in elementary school, it was really difficult for me. Almost everything I learned, I had to learn by listening and commit to memory. My report cards always said that I was working below my grade level. I had to train myself to focus my attention. I became very visual and learned how to create mental images in order to comprehend what I read. I found out early that you learn ways to compensate for what you are lacking.

A teacher in Steele Elementary School paid particular attention to my education and was very passionate about me receiving a quality education. In spite of being diagnosed with Dyslexia, she let me know that she still fully expected my best and she always showed me that she cared about me as a person. She was also determined that I would not be let down in my education. When the school district wanted to put me in an un-graded classroom, this teacher went above and beyond by assisting my mom to make sure I stayed in mainstream classrooms. Even in spite of all my struggles, she did not give up on me. Instead, she challenged me to work hard and to believe in myself. This teacher was Mrs. Alda Hanna, my 5th grade teacher at Steele Elementary. Mrs. Hanna retired in 1994 after teaching in the Harrisburg School District for 30 years.

Wildwood, NJ

In the summer, every few years, my mom and dad would take me to the beach and Morey's Piers Amusement Park in Wildwood, NJ. My cousin Derrick and I were only a year apart and we hung out together often. My parents used to always take Derrick with us so I would have someone my age to have fun with in Wildwood. If my parents had the extra money, sometimes we would spend a night at a motel in Wildwood and come back home the next day. One thing I can remember clearly is they always let Derrick and me ride on the Go Carts. The Go Carts were so much fun! Derrick and I used to race each other around the track and most of the time I would win the race. Even though Derrick will tell you he won most of the time. Then we would head to the beach to catch a couple waves as my mom and dad lay out on the beach. Then off to the arcades on the boardwalk we would go. It was always a fun time whenever we went to Wildwood.

As a kid growing up in Harrisburg, the Camp Curtin YMCA had always been my home away from home and it is still that way today. Every time I walked through those doors, I felt welcomed. As a kid, I always enjoyed playing on the basketball team, playing air hockey, swimming and shooting pool; I especially enjoyed lifting weights. It was always fun for me at the YMCA.

I had two father-figures at the YMCA in Donny Weaver and Greg Campbell. Greg was the basketball coach and he was very passionate about his role as the basketball coach. These two men helped to teach me how to be strong. They taught me how to play basketball against the best because they saw something in me that I didn't see in myself at the time. Weave and Campbell also showed me tough love when I needed it.

Basketball Challenge

I can remember playing basketball in my freshman year of high school and averaging 25 points a game. During this time, a good friend named Sean Broden supported me in sports like I was his little brother. In fact, on many occasions, I felt like we were brothers. Sean came to all my basketball games my freshman year. One time in particular, I remember in a basketball game in the Camp Curtin gymnasium, Sean sat under the basket where I could see and hear him throughout the game cheering me on to do something special. This was a game against our rival team, the Steel High Rollers, and it was a sell-out crowd. Above all the noise in the gym, I heard Sean shout, "Pint, you a get a dunk I will buy you some Jordan's". Now back then, a pair of Jordan's meant everything to me and my friends. In fact, I still love my Jordan's now, and its 2010!

The next time down the court, I had a fast-break and I tried to dunk the ball, but I missed. I turned to Sean and said, "Next time I get another fast-break, I'm gonna dunk it and I want those Jordan's." At the end of the game, my opportunity came again to dunk. I got a steal and was heading down the court on another fast-break all by myself. All I could hear was someone shouting "Get a dunk! Get a dunk!" So I just went as high as I could and dunked the ball with a little room to spare! Sean and the crowd went crazy yelling and screaming. After the game, I went up to Sean and gave him a chest bump. We won the game by two points that day. The next day, Sean and I went shopping for Jordan's. Ever since then, every time I dunked the ball in a game that year, Sean bought me a pair of brand new

sneakers. At the end of the season, I had five
pairs of new Jordan's in my closet.

Drugs & Alcohol

As a teenager, it was not easy for me to stay away from the drugs because it was all around me; even some of my friends were doing drugs and drinking beer and alcohol on a regular basis. But thankfully, doing drugs, drinking alcohol and smoking marijuana was not my thing. I kept myself busy by playing sports and focusing on my education. I am so thankful that I had great parents that were always there for me, and who loved me unconditionally. They were interested in what I was doing and wanted to know who I was hanging around with, especially my dad. A lot of people can't say that they have the support of their parents. But I can. That is what kept me grounded, along with my love for sports.

Hanging Out

My cousins Ronnie Daniels and Derrick Burke, and also my best friends Butchie and Barry always used to hang out together. We used to hang out at the Camp Curtin YMCA on N. 6th Street or get our dirt bikes and go riding around. My dad always made sure I had a basketball and a football so sometimes we played basketball on the basketball courts at the playground or played a game of football if we could round up enough guys to make it competitive.

I can remember when we used to always watch pro football and basketball games on TV at each other's houses. We would be glued to the TV cheering on our favorite teams. My favorite NBA team and NFL team were the Philadelphia Eagles and the Philadelphia 76ers, respectively. Both are Pennsylvania teams. My favorite players for the Philadelphia Eagles were:
•Wilbert Montgomery # 31, running back. He shattered almost all of the Eagles' rushing records and led the team in rushing six times. Montgomery was a powerful runner and it was amazing to see how fast he could run once he got the ball. The other Eagle player was:
•Harold Carmichael #17, wide receiver. At 6'8", Carmichael was one of the tallest wide receivers ever to play the game. Carmichael had some great hands and it was fascinating to watch him catch the ball over top of defenders and head down the sidelines for a touchdown. He was much more than a very dangerous red zone threat, he was tough, and a great blocker. Carmichael went on to play for 13 seasons with the Philadelphia Eagles.

My favorite players for the 76ers were:
•Maurice Cheeks aka Mo Cheeks, point guard. Mo was an all-time leader in steals for the 76ers.
•Julius Erving aka Dr. J. forward guard. I always enjoyed watching Dr. J. He was an all-around great player. Dr. J. once said, "Goals determine what you're going to be." That

statement is so true in life because if you don't have any goals, you will surely get lost along the way.

Their favorite NFL team was the Dallas Cowboy and we would make small bets that our team would win. When our team won, one of us would have to buy the other a candy bar or a soda.

These were guys I always knew I could count on and trust. I knew they would always have my back no matter what the circumstances. They have always been there for me since we were small kids and have always shown me mad love. That's why I wish the best for all of them.

CHAPTER 3

Tragedy Struck

In high school, I had a successful freshman year as a running back and as a point guard on the basketball team. My grades were not the best but I was studying really hard and was hanging in there. My future was looking bright. I was looking forward to my sophomore year in high school.

But then, tragedy struck my household. In my sophomore season in high school, my dad died suddenly of a massive heart attack at the age of 36. His death hit me especially hard because it was so sudden. Actually, my dad had just dropped me off that morning for my first practice on the varsity squad at Harrisburg High. How could he be dead by that afternoon? When my uncles came to the high school to get me and tell me of my dad's death, I could not accept it. I was close to both of my parents and I could not believe this was happening. I was really struggling to keep it together. After going through a serious bout of depression, I was determined to get it together. My mom was devastated in the loss of my dad, and I tried to be strong for her. It was a rough time for both of us, but my grandpop and other family members were there for me and my mom with their love and support. They did whatever needed to be done for us. My dad died on August 15, 1988. I was sixteen years old. It was just me and my mom now.

I remembered the lessons my mom and dad had taught me, and the values they instilled in me ever since I was a young boy. So even though my dad would never see me play a varsity football game, I knew he would have wanted me to finish what I started, and continue to be the best I could be as a person and as an athlete. So even though accepting the death of my dad was the hardest thing I ever had to do, I also knew what I had to do.

I was inspired by my dad's memory and I carried him in my heart in every classroom and in every game I played. Even though my dad was now deceased, I still wanted to continue to make him and my mom proud of me, as I tried to become the respectable and competitive and young man my parents had raised me to be.

PART THREE

Robert Tate

CHAPTER 4

High School

I was doing great on the basketball court and on the football field at Harrisburg High School. People used to tell my mom and dad that when I got to high school, I was going to get all the ink, and I sure did. I was in our local newspaper, The Patriot News, almost every week. People at my school began to call me, "Mr. Harrisburg." Sadly though, my dad never had the chance to read any news articles about me in the newspaper. I know he would have been so proud.

Many people that I was close to didn't know that when I played high school freshmen football, I had my doubts about whether or not I was really good enough to compete with the rest of these guys because I was so small. I was like 5'10, 165 pounds in a wet suit, really. But what made me look good was my speed. I was always a little faster than the other guys and that was because I was afraid to get tackled. I just ran as fast as I could with the football in my hand so the players could not tackle me. When I was playing in Little League Football, I was always on the defensive side of the ball, but then as a high school freshman, I was on the offensive side of the ball, where it is always probable that you would get tackled, hard. But after a while, I actually got used to being tackled. Of course I still ran as fast I could trying to get that almighty touchdown! Overall, playing freshman football was fun and that's what I did. I had fun and I had a great time doing so. Even though most of my time was spent running down the football field like a chicken with his head cut off, trying to be elusive and not to get tackled. Like I said before, I was 5'10" 165 pounds in a wet suit.

It was always fun for me playing football because the game was so competitive and I enjoyed the game so much, but as much as I enjoyed playing football, basketball was my true love. I was very passionate about basketball and I got great satisfaction and pleasure in playing the game. Everyone who knew me by my nickname of Pint back in Harrisburg, PA thought I was going to one day be a professional basketball player. They saw how good I was and they saw the passion I had for the game and my commitment to the game. Not one person thought I would become a professional football player.

Everyone used to tell me I was good, just like my dad was in basketball (he was 6'1" and 190 pounds). I really loved the game and I had high hopes and dreams of making it to the NBA one day. But deep down inside I knew that no matter how good my skills in basketball were, my height would keep me out of the NBA. So I focused my energy on football in hopes of one day going to the NFL. My mom was hoping that if I went to college, I would choose to play basketball, because she said you don't get knocked around as much in basketball as you do in football. Even in little league football, my mom always feared that I would get hurt. My dad would always reassure her by saying, "He's a tough one, my son will be alright."

I can remember in a home-game my junior year of high school against Cedar Cliff; tight end Kyle Brady came from out of no where and tackled me from behind. I went down hard. The air went out of me as I hit the ground. I was lying on the field for a few seconds trying to get myself together when I looked up and there was my mom, on the field, with worry written all over her face asking me if I was okay. I said, "Yes, I'm okay and mom, you shouldn't be on this football field." After all, I was a premier running back; I did not need to have my mom on the football field making sure I was alright. I had to keep my image intact. I guess you can call it "a guy thing."

Sylvan Learning Center

When I entered junior high school, I was still struggling academically, and it was very frustrating for me but somehow I managed to keep my head just above water. I had to attend summer school just about every year so that I could bring up my grades and be able to pass to my next grade. I hated going to summer school but I did what I had to do so that I could play sports. In sports, I excelled and did great things in the game. I often wondered why I couldn't do the same thing in the classroom. My parents helped and they also had to get me a tutor to help me with my school work on a regular basis.

After my dad died my mom enrolled me in the Sylvan Learning Center part-time after school. Since I was dyslexic, an education expert at Sylvan gave me an in-depth assessment to find out my exact learning needs. After that was established, a lesson plan was developed for me. With the guidance of trained and qualified tutors at Sylvan, my academics significantly improved. Sylvan's focus was on giving me the confidence I needed to achieve inside the classroom and their educational services are tailored for each individual student.

My confidence level in the classroom was increased by more than 50% in my first two weeks at Sylvan. I was really motivated and actually looked forwarded to going to my Sylvan tutor sessions. My grades were improving from D's and F's to C's and D's and I was beginning to feel quite proud of myself academically. My mom was really impressed with my progress inside the classroom. She told me that Sylvan's highly personalized approach to learning was exactly what I needed at that time to help get me on track.

Enrolling me in the Sylvan Learning Center was the best thing my mom could have done for me. With the specialized way of learning that Sylvan taught me, for the first time, I was finally able to do okay in school and my self-confidence in the classroom reached a really high level. It never reached the confidence level I felt when I was on the football field or the basketball court but I was feeling pretty good about myself when I received my test score grades of a C or maybe a D and once in a great while, I even was somehow able to achieve a B! I attended the Sylvan Learning Center for two years.

High School Coaches

In high school football, I was pushed hard by a good mentor/coach and a good friend/coach named Roy Purdy. He was always there for me when things were hard and not going the way I would have liked it to go. Coach Purdy always said, "No pain, no gain." But then again, I guess everyone would like things to be easy. However, I learned that in life, it just doesn't work that way.

I also had a great Head Coach in high school named Coach Earl Mosley. He taught me a lot about playing the game of football; not just with my speed, but also with smarts. He used to say, "Football is about angles and until you are able to get that, you are not going to be good enough to play football at a Division I University." Coach Mosley always let me know

51

that football was not everything and that my education should always come first. He said he saw such raw talent in me, that he knew for sure that I would be successful on the football field, but he let me know he was beginning to become a little concerned about me in the classroom. So he made sure I had tutors to help me stay on top of my grades.

I enjoyed being in high school at Harrisburg High. I was very outgoing and had no problems making friends. However, I was still a little shy when it came to the girls. I became an All-American running back in high school. I rushed for over 1,000 yards three times in my high school career. I lettered in four sports for two years; I played football, basketball, baseball and ran Track. I won gold medals in track in the 100 yard dash and as the anchor in the 4x4 200 meter relays.

In my sophomore year, I met and began talking to a young lady named Sherita Jackson who also attended Harrisburg High School and was on the band front. She and I hit it off really well and by the time I was a junior, Sherita and I were dating. I brought her home to meet my mom and Thomas and it was all good. I was Sherita's date for her senior prom that year. The next year, she was my date for my senior prom.

My Senior Year of High School

In my yearbook I was voted most popular and most athletic. I was selected to play in the Big 33 Football Classic which is always played in Hershey at the Hershey Park football field. This game is considered the Super Bowl of high school football and I was honored to be selected to play. Every year in the NFL Super Bowl game, there is at least one alumnus from the Big 33 Classic football game. So you can imagine how happy I was to be nominated and selected to play in the game. The Big 33 Football Classic would be played in July in Hershey.

Later that school year, I was also selected to play in the McDonald's All-American High School Basketball Game. Being selected as a McDonald's All-American instantly brands a basketball player as one of the top high school players in the United States. The teams are sponsored by McDonald's, the fast-food chain. It was quite an honor to be nominated and selected to play for this game also. The game would be played in April. Things were really looking great for me! But unfortunately, I did not play in either game.

Academically Ineligible

You see, even though I was selected to play in the McDonald's All-American High School Basketball game, I could not play in the game because in the middle of the basketball season, I was ruled academically ineligible to play basketball. By the time I became eligible to come back to the basketball team, the deadline had already passed for me to play on the McDonald's All-American team. I was crushed. I loved basketball. To be denied the opportunity to play in the championship game of high school hoops really hurt deep.

I was selfishly angry at my teachers, I was angry at my coaches, I was angry at everyone, for this predicament I found myself in. I remember getting so mad, that I threw my book in my classroom that I had failed in. They said the book hit my teacher on her leg, but that certainly was not my intention. I was just so angry and frustrated that I threw the book in the classroom, never intending for the book to hit anyone. I apologized to the teacher in person and in writing because I felt so bad. However, assault charges filed against me for this act and I had to appear before the District Justice Magistrate. My mom and the Athletic Director, Fred Clark secured the services of Attorney, Corky Goldstein to represent me at the hearing. However, after one day of being on the stand, and both counsel talking to each other during recess, the charges against me were dropped. I walked out of the District Justice office with a clean record.

To this day, that incident has stayed with me and I am truly sorry that the book hit my teacher on the leg; I never meant to hurt anyone.

Finally, after a few days of sulking, I became angry at myself for not working as hard in my studies as I should have. As a result, I accepted the fact that being ruled academically ineligible to play basketball and missing the opportunity to play in the McDonald's All-American games was the consequence I had to pay.

While I was still wallowing in my self-pity, I heard a voice in the back of my head saying, "You are always going to be faced with challenges through-out life; it is how you deal with these challenges that will determine if you will succeed in life. You will need to face these challenges head-on and deal with them in order to be able to move past it." My mom told me that a long time ago and now in my head, I heard her voice saying it to me again. I worked hard and brought those two "D's" that made me academically ineligible, up to a "C". It was hard, really hard, but I did it. It was still too late for me to play in the McDonald's All Star game, but I was able to finish the basketball season.

I was still eligible to play in the Big 33 Football Classic but in spite of my football coaches, Athletic Director Fred Clark (who I was very close to and he was like a father figure to me in high school) and everyone else persistently trying to get me to play in the Big 33, I still would not budge from my decision not to play. In the end, Fred Clark told me to just follow my heart. I felt if I could not play for the McDonald All-Star game to represent my school, I would not play in the Big 33 to represent my school either. I know that does not make sense now, but that was my reasoning back then. My mom used to tell me I had a stubborn streak in me and sometimes I was too stubborn for my own good. But did I ever regret my decision not to play in the Big 33 Football Classic? The answer is, "In hindsight, I believe I may have made too hasty of a decision not to play in the Big 33." But at the time, I thought I had made the right decision. I chalk it up as another life-lesson learned.

My Mom's New Boyfriend

Before becoming academically ineligible, I was angry at my mom for having a new boyfriend. I felt that the only man that really loved my mom was my dad, no one else. I did not want any other man being a part of our life. When I found out my mom was dating, I was hurt. My mom said, she still loved my dad but life must go on, for me and for her. She said she was not trying to replace my dad with someone else because she loved my dad and he could never be replaced. I did not understand.

My mom's new boyfriend was Thomas Washington from Baltimore. I knew nothing about him and I did not care to know anything about him. I just knew I did not want him around our family and he was never going to be a part of our family. I tried everything to show disrespect to Thomas so he would go away. But sadly, in the process, I was disrespecting my mom too because I began playing hooky from school, and staying out all night and not calling home and finally I just left home all together and began staying with friends. Sometimes, I would sneak back home in the mornings after my mom went to work to get some clothes and to eat a little something. But I would not stay. I knew that it was wrong but at the time, I just didn't care. This went on for several weeks.

When I finally came back home to stay, the kindhearted person that my mom is, she welcomed me back into our home. But she also told me I need to get my behind back in school. Thomas tried to talk to me to reassure me he had no intention of ever hurting my mom or our family because he truly cared about my mom and me. But at that time, I just did not believe him. However, my mom still continued to date him. I began to slowly let my guard down, just a little bit. I cautiously began taking baby steps to accept Thomas into our family, but this was a big adjustment for me. As time went on, the baby steps went to larger steps and after a while, I began to kind of like Thomas. We began talking more and doing things together which was good for the both of us. He also assured me that it was not his intention to try to take my dad's place. He just wanted us to be friends. In the process of our communications, we became closer and closer and began to build a relationship. I started seeing my mom smiling more often which made me feel really good. It took my mom a long time to smile again after my dad's death, so this was good to see. My mom seemed genuinely happy with Thomas and it felt so good for me to see my mom happy.

My Mom Became a Foster Parent

Before my mom met Thomas, I had to adjust to her becoming a foster parent. She was a foster mother to a two-year old girl named Mariah. I was used to being the only child for all these years, now I had to share my mom's attention with somebody else. She said I was out of the house so much being involved with sports, it was getting lonely and empty in the house. So she wanted to care for a young child that needed her nurturing. It took me a little while, but I got used to having a small child in our house. That's when along came Thomas.

Today, Thomas and I are really close and I love and respect him. He's treats me just as if I was his natural born son and he treats my mom with love, kindness and the respect she deserves.

My Senior Prom

I attended my senior prom with my girlfriend Sherita. I rented a black tuxedo with a white shirt and light pink Cummerbund to match Sherita's very pretty floor-length light pink gown. She really looked pretty in her gown. When I brought Sherita home so that my mom and Thomas could see us before we went to the prom, I thought my mom and grandpop would never stop taking pictures of us. We were finally able to leave the house in the Lincoln Towne Car that Thomas had rented for me to use for prom night. Sherita and I drove to the Ramada Hotel in Camp Hill, PA to attend our prom festivities in the beautifully decorated Banquet Hall and to take more pictures!

My Senior Year

In my senior year, I was heavily recruited by more than 20 Division I colleges such as Florida, Michigan, Wisconsin, Pittsburgh, Virginia Tech, Kentucky, and others. They were all offering me full athletic scholarships for football and basketball. I was invited to attend their colleges to see their campus and meet their athletic staff. Each school was hoping I would sign a Letter of Intent to accept a scholarship to attend their college when I graduated from high school. However, late in my senior year, I had a lot to worry about. I did not score high enough on my SAT and that scared many colleges away. My hopes of receiving a scholarship to a Division I College began to slowly fade away.

My high school coach recommended that after I graduated, I should enroll in a prep school. He said attending a prep school could help me to boost up my GPA when I went to college. He said a prep school could also help prepare me to take the SAT again to get a higher score and be able to still receive a scholarship to a Division I College. I felt hurt and was a little bit embarrassed, well, a whole lot embarrassed about not being able to receive a scholarship right now. After all, my senior year I was an All-League, All-Pennsylvania and All-American player being highly recruited for football and basketball by more than 20 Division 1 colleges. Now instead of going to college, here I was considering going to a prep school. It just did not make sense. Everyone was asking me what college was I going to and I had no answer for them. I felt I had let myself, my mom and everyone else down.

I began having doubts about myself again, but instead of these doubts pulling me down, this time it helped to motivate me. I learned that we all have doubts about our abilities and our chance for success but it's how we react to those doubts that matter. It would be wonderful thing if we had complete confidence in every decision or challenge we took on, but that's not reality. Even the most accomplished people in society have doubts. But they never let the doubts prevent them from succeeding; instead, they embrace the doubts and use them as motivation. That's what I did.

High School Graduation

Graduation day had finally arrived. That morning I got up early and my mom fixed a hearty breakfast for everyone. My mom was so happy for me. She said nothing in this world could keep her away from seeing me walk across the stage to accept my high school diploma. Mom and Thomas were so proud of me. I was proud of myself too, but I was not happy about not being able to get a higher score on the SAT. After graduation, I was not sure what I was going to do. I couldn't go to a Division 1 College on an athletic scholarship, in fact, all the colleges stopped talking and corresponding with me. I knew I had the skills to be able to play basketball or football in college. I just needed to score higher on the SAT which was very hard for me because I did not test well. Mom began to dress my little foster sister Mariah so she could attend my graduation with her and Thomas. As I continued to get dressed myself, I was beginning to feel a little better as I thought about this accomplishment in my life; I was about to become a 1992 high school graduate! I smiled to myself, got dressed and told mom and Thomas that I would see them at the graduation ceremony. Mom gave me a hug and a kiss and told me again how very proud she was of me. Thomas gave me some dap and told me to keep my head up. He also said he was proud of me too. I drove to the high school with some friends.

The Commencement Exercises were held for my high school graduation in June 1992 on our school's football field. I proudly walked across the stage to accept my high school diploma. Mom and Thomas were so proud of me as I walked across that stage. My mom said her heart was filled with pride and joy that I had graduated from high school. It was very emotional for her. After all, this was a day that my mom had been told by my school counselors would most likely never happen for me. But this time, they were dead wrong. At the age of 20, I was a 1992 high school graduate and it felt great! I had beat the odds!

I had to leave my graduation before the graduation ceremony was over to catch a flight to compete in the Penn Relays Track Meet in California. This was where the top ranked track and field runners throughout the country were competing. Our high school 4x4 relay team had qualified for this all-star event four weeks previous at a track meet in Shippensburg. Marvin, Urutia and Lincoln who were my three classmates from the 4x4 relay team, left our graduation with our track coach, Coach Cameron. He took us to the Harrisburg International Airport to catch our flight. We returned home two days later with the Gold Medal for the 4x4 Relay Race. I was the anchor.

New Additions to our Family

After my mom took care of her two-year old foster daughter Mariah for three months, she was returned home to her parents. However, it did not take long for mom to become a foster mother again. Two weeks after Mariah went home, mom received a phone call again from Dauphin County Children & Youth asking if she could take care of two more foster children; two sisters named Larese and Shaniece, ages two and four. Of course mom said yes. Our family keeps growing. These two girls would remain with mom and Thomas for seven years before being returned home to their mother.

Robert Tate

CHAPTER 5

Milford Academy

Mom, Thomas and I had a long talk about me attending Milford Academy and about challenges in my life and how I would have to handle them. I knew they were right, plus, I knew that is what my dad would have wanted me to do too. So two weeks after graduation, I went to Milford Academy for my initial Admissions Interview process to see if Milford Academy and I would prove to be a good fit. I met with the dean, the teachers and the coaching staff. It was a very interesting meeting. Milford Academy let me know that 92% of its students went on to colleges. But they were very proud of the fact that more than two thirds of their graduates received full four-year scholarship offers!

They said their students typically represent a diverse range of backgrounds. Many of these students are gifted athletes who have the opportunity to attain four-year athletic scholarships at major universities throughout the country but are having problems academically with making the grade or get a high enough SAT score. They also said that over the years, Milford Academy has established a successful track record in helping these student athletes meet their goals. Their classes are small, enabling each teacher well-versed in his or her particular field to devote more time to the individual student's scholastic needs. The dean said in selecting a student for admission to Milford Academy, the Academy considers not only a student's high school grades, and college board scores, but also his/her:

▪Motivation to pursue an undergraduate or postgraduate year

▪Potential to succeed and graduate from Milford Academy

▪Athletic ability (if pursuing a collegiate athletic scholarship)

▪Character as an individual

▪Ability to flourish in a competitive environment

They said my one-year experience at Milford Academy Prep School would be very intense and that I would learn a lot in a short period of time, one year to be exact. They would do everything they could to help me succeed and to prepare me for my SAT, but most of it would be on me. They said with my hard work and dedication to my education, they saw no reason why I couldn't increase my GPA and score higher on the SAT and still be able to attend a Division 1 college on a full athletic scholarship. I came home quite impressed with Milford Academy.

The next week my mom received a letter in the mail that I had been accepted to attend Milford Academy. It looked like I had a second chance. But this chance would cost $12,000 for my tuition. I was offered a partial football scholarship to attend Milford Academy.

My mom and Thomas put on a Talent Showcase fundraiser event to raise money for the rest of the tuition and they did great! They raised $3500 from the Talent Showcase and my grandpop gave my mom the rest of the money! Two weeks later, with mom's and Thomas' blessings, I enrolled in Milford Academy Prep School, in Milford, CT.

My Daughter Is Born

One month after I enrolled in Milford Academy, my high school sweetheart and I became the proud parents of a baby girl. Sherita gave birth to our daughter, a beautiful baby girl named Shekia Lakay Tate. She was born on August 9, 1992 in Polyclinic Medical Center. When I saw my daughter for the first time, she was so tiny and beautiful. I was afraid to hold her. But I did hold her and told her that daddy was here and that I loved her. That was seventeen years ago, and now she is a senior in high school!

After being home for a week and spending time with my newborn daughter, I went back to Milford Academy and worked extra hard in my studies. By now I was used to having to work three times harder than everyone else. But I did it because that is what I needed to do if I wanted to make the grade. Along with working hard in the classroom, I also played on the basketball team as a "walk-on" point guard and on the football team as a running back and I excelled in both. I scored 19 touchdowns and rushed for over 1,000 yards in football.

My first love had always been basketball and I truly loved the game. But I decided that because of my modest height of 5'11", I would stand a better chance of getting drafted into the NFL after college rather than the NBA. There are only about 58 guys each year that get drafted into the NBA, but there are about 240 guys that get drafted each year in the NFL draft. So I knew that if I received an athletic scholarship for college, it would have to be for football.

I continued to take SAT preparatory classes and near the end of the school year at Milford Academy, I took the SAT again. I thought I did okay but I just was not sure. But I was anxious to know how I did. However, I was told the results of my SAT score would be mailed to my house at 2309 N. 6th Street, Harrisburg. I knew this SAT score did not define me as a person or what my character was. But I knew that I needed to score higher on this SAT to reach my goal. After attending school for one year, I graduated from Milford

Academy Prep School with a 2.9 GPA which I worked very hard for! Two weeks later, my mom said the letter with my SAT score had come in the mail. I casually asked her, "Did I pass it?" I was very nervous, because I had a lot riding on whether or not I had passed my SAT. My mom said she did not open it. She said, "I was waiting for you to come home, so that you could open it."

I opened the letter very slowly. I took the letter out of the envelope, I carefully unfolded the letter and read it and saw my score. I had passed my SAT with a score of 890! I needed a 750. The highest score was 1500. But I was definitely happy with my 890! This score had opened back up some doors for me that had been closed when I graduated high school. Mom was in seventh heaven, Thomas was really glad for me and I was on cloud nine!! Oh happy days!

One month later, I signed a Letter of Intent to attend the University of Cincinnati on a full four-year football athletic scholarship. I had determinedly remained focused and was rewarded for all my hard work by receiving a full athletic scholarship to a Division 1 College.

Robert Tate

CHAPTER 6

University of Cincinnati

From the first day I stepped onto the University of Cincinnati campus, I felt right at home. I knew I would do well here, plus I was very happy to be here. I met the academic staff and then the football coaching staff. The head football coach was Rick Minter. I was ready to work hard in my studies and to play college football.

Since I had always played several sports in school, I tried to play basketball at Cincinnati as a walk-on, but academically, it just didn't work out for me to play both sports. School work in college was a lot harder than high school and I could not manage two sports plus stay academically eligible. Since I was already there on a football scholarship, I put all my heart into studying and playing football.

As a freshman in college, I practiced at cornerback, tailback, and receiver. I had one of the top weight room performances with a vertical jump of 35 inches, the 40-yard-dash in 4.40 and the 20-yard-dash in 2.60. My first game as a freshman was against Austin Peay, which we won 42-10. In this game I saw action on the special teams. My third game was against Tulsa at our home field in Nippert Stadium where we also won 22-15. I demonstrated my athletic versatility and earned Prep Team Offensive Player of the Week. In our 4th game, we lost against Syracuse by a score of 24-21.

In my sophomore year, I got a whole lot better. I had a strong pair of hands when it came to catching the ball and I had the ability to stay focused under pressure. It was nearly impossible to tear the ball away from me once I got a hold of it. I think Coach Minter noticed this too, because during my sophomore season, I was switched from running back to wide receiver for the Bearcats; along with continuing my duties as a kick return specialist.

Mom and Thomas Got Married

Back home, On August 27, 1994, my mom got married again and Thomas Washington became my step-father. The wedding ceremony was held at Macedonia Missionary Baptist Church. I was proudly a part of the wedding party as one of the groomsmen, along with my two foster sisters Larese and Shaniece as flowers girls. They had a pretty big wedding and once again, my mom looked lovely in her wedding gown with her little belly showing just a little bit because she was four months pregnant at the time. My grandpop gave my mom away.

Five months later, my brother, Spencer Thomas Washington was born. He was born on January 19, 1995. (My brother and I are 23 years apart). I told my mom I always wanted a brother, I just didn't know I would finally get one when I was in my second year of college!

Back to School

Back in college; I continued to have a very good season and began to make a name for myself on the football field. I was now the starting wide receiver and was named Conference USA Offensive Player of the Year and Special Teams Player of the Year. In a game against Tulsa that year, I returned the second-half kickoff 88 yards for a touchdown as Cincinnati won the game 24 to 5.

After an outstanding season playing for the Bearcats, I began to really believe I might actually have a shot at playing in the NFL. Coach Minter said I was their go-to guy when they needed points. He said, "It's going to be our mission to get the ball to Tate as many times and ways as we can. For Tate to touch the ball 70 to 80 times will be a minimum figure we are going to strive for."

As a sophomore, I caught 46 passes for 895 yards and five touchdowns, which were the most yards in a season for a UC receiver since Tom Ross accumulated 1,021 in 1968. In the classroom I still struggled but I always had a tutor which was a big help to me.

In 1996, when I was a junior, I was scouted in college because of my outstanding abilities on the football field, and was invited to the NFL Combines the next year.

I led the nation in kickoff returns averaging 34.3 yards per return, including one for a touchdown. I averaged 8.2 yards per punt return and rushed seven times for 35 yards. My 1,685 all-purpose yards set a school record. For my outstanding season, I was the recipient of The Claude Rost Most Valuable Player Award.

People began telling me I should enter the NFL Draft. I was putting up big numbers as a wide receiver that looked very good. Some NFL analysts on TV were saying if I entered the draft now, I would most likely be taken in the third or fourth round.

However, I thought that if I stayed in college one more year, my stats would go up my senior year. Then when I declared myself eligible for the draft; I would possibly be drafted higher. Plus, unlike the NBA, the NFL was not drafting many underclassmen, and I wasn't sure I would be drafted if I left school early. After talking to my mom and Thomas about the draft, I made the decision to stay in college at the University of Cincinnati for my senior year. My parents agreed with my decision. They said when I received my degree in Business Communications; no one could ever take it away from me. I also thought that by staying in college another year and getting more playing time, I would be both physically and mentally more prepared for the NFL.

I thought about when mom and Thomas drove me to Cincinnati three years ago. They were so excited for me, especially my mom, who kept saying, "My baby is going to college!" I was pretty excited too but I did not want to show it. I just wanted to remain cool, calm, and collected. When we arrived on campus, I went to the Athletic Director's office to meet with the coaches. Now here I was three years later, making this major decision of my life to stay in school another year.

My Senior Year at the University of Cincinnati

I lived in the dorms on campus my entire time at the University of Cincinnati. I had become friends with a lot of the guys on the football team including Sam Garnes and Anthony Ladd who later played in the NFL. We hung out together sometimes after football practice and played some hoops. I was a quiet person. I did not drink or use any type of drugs. I did try smoking a cigarette once and almost choked to death, I never tried it again. I always said I was an athlete and did not have time for that other stuff. After each football game, I always tried to wear a suit and tie. I didn't want people to see me only as a football player; I also wanted them to know I was a student. My senior year finally rolled around. I was working hard in the classroom and my grades were looking pretty good. Soon, it was football season again.

Bus Trip

My mom chartered a bus to Cincinnati on my 24th birthday so family and friends could come see me play for the Bearcats and afterwards; help me to celebrate my birthday. My position was wide receiver and my jersey number was 83. Everyone was excited to see me play. I scored two touchdowns and my family went wild! I was really happy to see Sherita and my daughter Shekia in the stands.

My Aunt Helen Holmes-Grier was in the stands too; she is an avid football fan and my mom told me she was in the stands giving our Bearcat cheerleaders some competition as she was "loudly" cheering me and the Bearcats to victory! My aunt Helen is one of my biggest football fans. By the time the game was over, she was hoarse from cheering so much. We all met up after the game was over and I joined everyone in their hotel banquet hall where my mom and Thomas had a birthday party for me.

Choosing an Agent

In college, I had begun to be recruited by a lot of sports agents wanting to become my agent in the event that I went Pro. They were writing to me at college, they were calling and writing my parents at home and a couple even came knocking at my door. After my list was narrowed down to two agents, I finally chose Ron Delduca to be my agent. Something about Ron Delduca stood out from the rest. I also liked the idea that he only represents a few athletes at a time. That way, he could spend more individualized time handling my business and financial needs.

On The Football Field

In my senior year of football, of all things to have happened; I injured my ankle in a game against Purdue and had to be taken to the hospital. When my mom received the news that I got hurt on the football field and was taken to the hospital, she was really worried about me. Thomas was holding it together as he tried to calm her down. My mom kept calling the hospital in Cincinnati to see how I was doing but was not getting any answers. She told Thomas they would have to drive to Cincinnati to see about me. I was finally able to call home to let my mom know that I was okay. I told my mom she and Thomas did not need to drive to Cincinnati, that I would be okay and would call them back later that day. They kept me in the hospital overnight and to my mom's relief, I was released the next day.

I could not believe this would happen again, but later in the season I had another major injury! This one was a well-publicized neck injury. I was on the injured reserve list for two weeks. When the NFL scouts came to the Bearcats game, I was sitting on the bench.

77

As bad as this injury was, it was not as bad as injuring my ankle earlier this football season. My neck still hurt a little, but I was able to move it real good. But my ankle just did not get right. The problem was that I could run straight but it was hard for me to turn on it. I couldn't come out the cuts like I used to and therefore, I was unable to gain extra yardage. In my three previous seasons, I never got hurt on the field. But now in my senior year, I have two major injuries in the same season. I thought to myself, "How did things go so wrong?"

If I would have taken a chance and left college to enter the NFL Draft my junior year, when I had an all-around great season, most analysts believed I would have been selected in the higher rounds of the draft. But I stayed in school. I got injured – my status for the NFL went down. Two months later, with my injured body and poor senior football season behind me, I declared myself eligible for the 1997 NFL draft.

Back home, mom and Thomas had adopted the two foster children they had been taking care of for the past three years. At that time, Tasha was six and Jasmine was eight.

The Senior Bowl Game

Although I was still not at 100%, in January 1997, I flew to Mobile, Alabama to play in the Senior Bowl Game. The Senior Bowl is an all-star annual college game that is held every January in Mobile, Alabama. Rosters consist of the top senior NFL Draft prospects in the nation.

Each year two NFL coaches are chosen to lead the North and South squads and they are responsible for selecting the rosters for each squad. It was an honor for me to be selected to play in this high-status game of collegiate sports. I was selected to play for the South squad. Our coach was Marty Schottenheimer, Head Coach of the Kansas City Chiefs.

The game was held at the Ladd-Peebles Stadium in Mobile. This game was televised on national TV and was played before a sellout crowd of 40,646. I returned two kickoffs for 57 yards, but our team lost to the North squad. The score was North 35 – South 14.

Prior to the game, the Senior Bowl photographer took pictures of each player that participated in the Bowl Game. They put the pictures on a card similar to a rookie card that had Senior Bowl Game written on it. It also had our number, the date and place of the game. They gave each player 100 copies of their Senior Bowl card.

A few notable alumni of the Senior Bowl include Joe Namath, Bo Jackson, Walter Payton, Steve McNair and Brett Favre.

Robert Tate

CHAPTER 7

NFL Scouting Combine

I attended the NFL Scouting Combine in February 1997. I really wanted to prove myself in the Combines. I thought this was my last chance to make a good showing for the NFL scouts. I was hoping I would do well enough in the Combines, to increase my chances of being drafted by the NFL.

In the Combines, it's almost like you are a piece of meat as they poke and prod you. However, many of the prospective NFL players have to go through this process. The Scouting Combine is usually held for one week in Lucas Oil Stadium in Indianapolis. The NFL prospects are put through a series of tests, drills, and interviews. More than 600 NFL personnel initiate these tests and drills, along with some head coaches, scouts, and general managers. They evaluate the nation's top college football players who are eligible for the NFL draft.

The Combine is very intense. All my years of high school football and college football came to this point – the Combine. You want your timing to be on and you want to do well in the interviews. In the interviews, you get the chance to let the interviewers know that you are ready to become a part of the NFL and what you have done to prepare yourself for the NFL. There is no time to be nervous; you just have to do what needs to be done. In your drills, they have to be spot on. I also had to pass a medical examination and a psychological examination which were administered by the NFL doctors.

Overall, I enjoyed participating in the Combines with a lot of other NFL hopefuls. I got the chance to meet a lot of great players and we had a good time. I also met a lot of NFL coaches, which made my time at the Combines special. I ran a 4.38 at the Combines. I just wanted to show the NFL coaches a sample of what I was capable of doing and that I belonged in the NFL.

The Combines is closed to the general public and the participants can attend by invitation only. Approximately 250 athletes attend the Combines each year. This year was no exception.

I left the Combine feeling pretty good about my performance. I thought I did what I came to do, which was prove to the Combine coaches that I belonged in the NFL.

PART FOUR

Robert Tate

Chapter 8

Drafted In the NFL

I was drafted as a wide receiver in the 6th round, the 183rd pick by the Vikings in the 1997 NFL Draft. This was a major accomplishment for me. At this point, all I wanted to do was make the team and prove to Coach Green that I was the right person for the job. After attending two weeks at a mini training camp working out and lifting weights in Minnesota, I attended a Rookie Symposium.

Rookie Symposium in Chicago

I attended an NFL-sponsored symposium in suburban Chicago for rookies that covered topics like drugs, alcohol, sex, financial management and life after football. The symposium was an eye-opening experience for me. In this symposium, the speakers talked a lot about drugs and alcohol. They spoke about living a whole new lifestyle when you play football for the NFL. They told us how girls will be pushing themselves upon us because we are professional athletes and that we have to be careful. They told us these types of girls are usually called groupies. With our jobs comes a lifestyle that many of us are not used to. The rookies that attended this symposium were listening very intently, including me. I knew a few of the rookies; many of them I had played against in college. There were about 200 rookies that had just been drafted and attended this symposium.

There were several speakers and they spoke to us on many topics, including our large NFL salaries. After all, many of these rookies that were picked in round 1 of the NFL Draft had become instant millionaires after being drafted. At this point, being drafted in the 6th round of the Draft, I was not one of them but it definitely felt great being here. The speakers talked about handling our money in a responsible manner because we will not be in the NFL forever. They also talked about partying. They said we should not party too much, lose focus of our goals, or get into trouble because NFL teams do not want trouble makers who like to get drunk and do stupid things or players who always get in trouble with the law. The speaker said if you want to make it in the NFL, stay out of trouble and keep partying to a minimum. If your friends are trouble makers you need to get new friends. But they could not stress enough that we should stay out trouble!

He said unfortunately, just because we were drafted, it did not mean we would automatically make the team; and those of us who made the team might only last a year in the NFL while some of us would last many years. They told us the only thing that was guaranteed about the NFL was our signing bonus because we get that upfront. We need to plan for the future when we are no longer making a high figure salary. And hopefully, when we leave the NFL, we will have a tidy little nest egg saved up. This symposium was a great experience and I felt I learned a lot in those two days.

Making the Team

I returned to Minnesota and attended the Viking Training Camp in Mankato, Minnesota. It was very intense. As I was working out, doing drills and catching footballs, the only thing that constantly stayed in the back of my mind was making the team. Thankfully, I made it through the first round of cuts in July.

In August, the final cuts had been made and I found out that I made the Vikings roster! That was one of the happiest days of my life! I had made it all the way from Little League Football to the NFL and it felt great! I wish my dad was here to share this moment with me. Coach Green pulled me into his office and said, "We expect a lot out of you, you're gonna have the opportunity to help us out a whole lot, just stay in shape."

I said, "Yes sir, I will."

Another Death in The Family

My grandpop, Richard Burnett, Sr. had attended many of my little league football games and high school football games. When I went to college, he especially used to enjoy traveling to Cincinnati with my mom and Thomas to watch me play college football. He never gave his advice on what I should do in the game, he just enjoyed watching me play the game. I respected that. But he never got the chance to see me play pro ball.

He was hospitalized in the Hershey Medical Center for about two weeks for something that had to do with his kidneys. He never came back home. He passed away in his sleep on January 3, 1997, four months before the NFL Draft. Dealing with my grandpop's death was quite emotional for me because my grandpop and I were close and we used to talk all the time. My mom took his death pretty hard because they were very close also. My mom even moved my grandpop in with us after he got his kidney transplant so she could help take care of him. He lived with us for several months. We lost a kind and wonderful man on that cold day in January. I wish he could have seen me play at least one NFL game. I know that would have made him so happy. But I knew that my grandpop and my dad would be smiling down upon me as I continue on my journey in football.

My paternal grandparents Harry Tate, Sr. and Mattie Tate passed away when I was in my pre-teen years. I know they too were looking down and smiling upon me.

Robert Tate

CHAPTER 9

The National Football League

The Minnesota Vikings

Pre-Season Hall of Fame Game – July 26, 1997

I had always wanted to visit Canton, Ohio and the Hall of Fame throughout my college career, but for one reason or another, I never made it. So I was very excited when the Vikings toured the Pro Football Hall of Fame and watched some highlight films on July 25, 1997. We were scheduled to play the Seattle Seahawks the next day. I could hardly believe it. Here I was, not only going through the Hall, but I was actually getting ready to play my first pre-season NFL game in Canton!

I can still remember the excitement of playing in a pre-season opener game against the Seattle Seahawks in the Hall of Fame Game. In this exhibition game, I gave the Viking offense good field position by returning five kickoffs for 169 yards, including a long run of 53 yards on the opening kickoff. It was a close game but we won with the score Vikings 28 Seahawks 26. My mom and Thomas drove to Ohio to attend my first NFL game. They were excited to see me play.

My First Apartment

I packed up and moved to Minnesota my rookie year. This was my first time moving into my own place and paying my own bills. Since I had always lived in the dorms at Milford Academy and the University of Cincinnati, this was a real experience for me. I moved into my very first apartment in Eden Prairie, Minnesota.

It was a very nice one bedroom apartment in an Apartment Complex located in an upscale neighborhood. I lived on the second floor. My apartment had all the amenities I needed at the time. It had central air, a washer and dryer, a dishwasher, a garbage disposal, a microwav, a balcony to sit out on and a parking garage. I was happy and contented with my apartment. For the first time in my life, I had to learn my way around in the kitchen a little bit. But I did not fool around with the stove much; most of my meals were take-out, or home delivery, fast food and Chinese food.

The first week of August, my mom and Thomas flew to Minnesota to visit me and to see how I was making out. They brought my little brother Spencer and my two foster sisters Tasha and Jasmine. My mom looked in my refrigerator and asked me what was I doing? There was nothing in it but Gatorade, juices, bottled water, lunch meat & cheese, milk and juices. When my mom looked in my cabinets, they did not look any better. There was nothing but junk foods like Tastycakes, chips, pretzels and candy. My mom asked Thomas to take her to the grocery store to buy some groceries so I could have a home-cooked meal for a change. I did not argue with that. My stove could sure use a workout.

My apartment was too small for everyone to stay so I put my mom, Thomas and my siblings up in a hotel near my apartment. I showed them around town and where the Vikings Camp was located. I also took them to the Mall of America, which is one of largest malls in the world. This mall has 400 stores in it. It even has an amusement park inside the mall, along with a 16-theatre movie theatre, a bowling alley and about 20 restaurants, plus several nightclubs. The Mall of America is located in the suburb of Bloomington in Twin Cities, Minnesota. Before leaving to fly back home, my mom told me to try to eat foods that were a bit more healthy. It was a nice visit with my family and Thomas and I joked about my mom having to cook me a meal. I drove everyone to the airport and we said our goodbyes for now. They said they would be back for my first home football game with the Vikings at the end of the month.

Later that year, my girlfriend Sherita and our daughter Shekia flew to Minnesota to spend time with me for Thanksgiving.

Robert Tate

My Rookie Year in the NFL

On August 31, 1997, with my mom and Thomas in attendance, I touched the ball for the first time in a regular season game. We played against the Buffalo Bills and I returned three kickoffs for 62 yards. We won my first NFL game 34-13. It was an incredible feeling to be playing football in the NFL. This was a whole new level of football and I was up to the challenge. I was ready to play some football!

In a game against the Green Bay Packers on Sunday, September 21, 1997, I was busy returning kick-returns. I hauled in four kickoffs for 77 yards including a return for 36 yards. The Vikings lost the game by a touchdown, Green Bay 38 – Vikings 32.

So far, I only had two catches for 20 yards as a wide receiver. With guys like Cris Carter and Jake Reed holding the starting spots, I knew I was going to have to earn my keep on special teams. Special teams was nothing new for me. I had led the nation in kickoff returns at the University of Cincinnati. So I knew what was in store; I just wanted to be ready. Special teams is the key for many guys who get drafted, that's what everyone usually plays first when they come into the league. You just have to keep playing until something happens. The main thing about the NFL, as I see it, is to learn the system. Learning the Vikings system meant learning Dennis Green's system. I was willing and ready to learn.

A Season Ending Injury

On September 28, 1997, only my fourth game in the NFL, I returned 10 kick returns for 196 yards before injuring my ankle in a 28-19 victory over the Philadelphia Eagles. I was placed on injured reserve the next week with a high-ankle sprain. I was expected to miss only a few weeks but I ended up being sidelined for the rest of the season! Coach Dennis Green said this type of sprain would take a long time to heal. The team doctors and Coach Green said if I expected my ankle sprain to heal up right, I needed to take my time coming back, instead of trying to rush back. I was devastated that I would have to sit out the rest of my rookie season. I spent the rest of the season focusing on healing my ankle. I did all kinds of therapy so I could be ready for next season. I was determined to get back in pads and back in the game. I thought I had a lot to offer the NFL and I hoped and prayed that I would not get cut before I had the chance to prove myself.

Disney World

During my first off-season, Sherita and I took our daughter Shekia to Disney World in Florida. Shekia really enjoyed it at Magic Kingdom theme park. She was amazed at seeing Minnie and Mickey Mouse up close and in person. Of course we had to buy her the

Mickey Mouse ears to wear. Shekia enjoyed riding all the kiddie rides in Magic Kingdom.

However, when my daughter was seven years old, her mother and I parted ways. Trying to maintain a long distance relationship after high school, had taken its toll on our relationship. I lived in Connecticut for a year attending Milford Academy; I then lived in Cincinnati for four years while attending the University of Cincinnati, while Sherita lived in Pittsburgh for four years attending Pittsburgh University. We spent time together during spring break and summer break. Even though we are no longer together, I will always respect Sherita. We shared and went through a lot together. However, the distance was our worst enemy. Sherita and I both have moved on with our lives.

My Second Year as a Viking

My ankle was 95% healed and I came back to the Viking lineup ready to play some football! I resumed my kickoff return duties. Our first game of the regular season was against the Tampa Bay Buccaneers. We won the game 31-7. I returned two kickoffs for 43 yards.

I stayed healthy and played in all 16 regular season games and two playoff games. This was our very best season yet. We had a record of 15-1 and were heading for the Super Bowl . . . at least we thought we were heading to the Super Bowl.

This was also the year that I received my NFL Rookie Card!

A Devastating Loss

The most disappointing loss for me as a Viking was on January 17, 1999 in the Metrodome in a championship game against the Atlanta Falcons. We were only one game away from the Super Bowl. Everything was going our way, we had home field advantage, our fans were fired up, and we were fired up. Our quarterback Randall Cunningham had enjoyed the greatest season of his career. He guided the Vikings to a 15-1 regular season record with 34 touchdown passes and only 10 interceptions. Cunningham had a good supporting cast that year, with All-Pro veteran Cris Carter, rookie sensation Randy Moss, Pro Bowl running back Robert Smith and me as kick-return specialist. Our All Pro kicker, Gary Anderson, had not missed a field goal the entire season, actually he had not missed in his last 45 attempts – but he missed the field goal attempt in the 4th Quarter.

We wanted to make history that year. All the TV sports analysts were saying no team had ever gone 15-1 in the regular season and not made it to the Super Bowl. If we made it to the Super Bowl, the Vikings would have made history with a black head coach and a black quarterback being in the Super Bowl for the first time. But it was not to be. We made history being the only NFL team to go 15-1 in the regular season and not make it to the Super Bowl. At the end of this game we were numb. There was a deafening quiet across the stadium. Nobody could believe we had just lost this game. The entire Vikings team was devastated, along with our fans. We lost that game by a field goal in overtime and the Falcons won the game. Falcons 30–Vikings 27.

In my third year with the Minnesota Vikings, something major happened and it was definitely for the better.

My Third Year in the NFL

In my third year in the NFL, things were looking good for me as a kick-returner and punt-returner, but I still was not getting much time as a wide receiver. I only had three catches for 16 yards. I was anxious to show my talent as a wide receiver, but sadly it was not to be. I still continued racking up yardage as a kick-return specialist as I waited for something to happen. In fact, something did happen.

My First Kickoff Return Touchdown

On Sunday, December 12, 1999, I recorded my first kickoff return for a touchdown! It happened in the second quarter against the Kansas City Chiefs when I returned a kickoff 76 yards for a Vikings touchdown! Gary Anderson's kick was good for the extra point. We were trailing the Chiefs 21-0 when I scored our touchdown. That touchdown put us on the scoreboard with the new score now Chiefs 21 – Vikings 7! Even though we went on to lose the game 31-28, that is a game I will never forget.

And something else happened too!

Switched From Wide Receiver to Cornerback

Early in December of 1999 as I headed to an 8:00 a.m. special teams meeting, I was called into Coach Green's office. I nervously walked down hallway to the coach's office as I wondered what the coach wanted to see me about. I began thinking that maybe I might be getting cut from the team. So I prepared myself for the worst. When I stepped into Coach Green's office, he got right to the point. He told me that I was being switched from wide receiver to cornerback, effective immediately. I just looked at Coach Green stunned! He told me that he believed I could make this transition. I immediately went to the Defensive Backs coach office and picked up a defensive playbook.

This move was bittersweet for me because I really wanted to showcase my skills as a wide receiver. I had prepared myself to work hard as I played on special teams as a kickoff returner and punt returner. Even though the Vikings still had a talented group of wide receivers in Chris Carter, Jake Reed and Randy

Moss, I knew my time would eventually come for me to play in the position of wide receiver. But now Coach Green was saying, "Let's switch your position." I was a little reserved about this change, because I knew I would have to start all over again to learn a new position and a new system. But I was willing to do whatever it took to continue playing in the NFL. If it meant playing the position of cornerback, then I was up for the challenge.

First Game As A Cornerback

I played my first game as a cornerback on December 20, 1999, against Brett Favre and the Green Bay Packers on Monday Night Football. I was a cornerback all of two weeks and here I was playing in a prime time game, on national television. To say it was an exciting time for me is an understatement. It was an incredible experience! I just prayed that I would not mess up. We won the game 24-20. This is what Kent Youngblood wrote about my first game as a cornerback:

> **Backed into a Corner – Tate showing Vikings he can play defensive back: by Kent Youngblood of the Minneapolis–St. Paul Tribune.**
> He wasn't scared. No, that's not the right word because Robert Tate wasn't afraid. Not even when the Minnesota Vikings coaches went up to him during pre-game warm-ups Monday night and informed him he would be playing cornerback in a

NFL game for the first time, on Monday night, prime time against the Green Bay Packers, in as crucial a game as the Vikings have played all season.

No fear? It was more than just a slogan. "No," Tate said. "There has to be another word for that. I wasn't scared. I wasn't nervous. There has to be another word. Excited? Enthused? Maybe. But I know I wasn't scared."

While we search the thesaurus, let's think of a word to describe what Tate did Monday night.

Stunning? Well, consider: A month ago Robert Tate, of Harrisburg, was a wide receiver, return man and specials teams whiz. Oh, and a survivor who had managed to stick on the Vikings' roster for three years by doing whatever the team asked him to do.

That said, it was still a stretch when they asked him to become a cornerback in the week before the December 6 game at Tampa Bay. And then, two weeks later, after Chris Rogers was hurt during pre-game warm-ups, they threw him into a game.

The result? Tate played in 51 plays, as the first extra defensive back on the field on passing downs. He did not get burned. He made a key tackle on Packers fullback William Henderson at the goal line, forcing a field goal try. And he almost had an interception when he stepped in front of a pass to receiver Bill Schroeder after reading a play. Unprecedented? "Well, that might never have happened before." Vikings defensive coordinator Foge Fazio said. There might have been an emergency, where somebody went back and finished a game. But I don't think anybody has ever been switched like that. It's extraordinary. It's unbelievable.

And it could happen again. Rogers is on the injury report as questionable because of a hamstring pull, meaning Tate could be the nickel-back again. And he knows this time will be tougher. The Giants will have a week to get ready, a week to figure out ways to take advantage of a first-time cornerback.

"I don't want to say too much. Because I only have one under my belt," Tate said. "But I'm not going to back down."

It's that mindset that got the Vikings thinking about making the switch in the first place. Tate, one of the fastest players on the team, did some scout team work at cornerback all season, and showed a flare for it. He has proven to be a strong tackler on special teams. After the switch, Solomon and Tate spent hours in two-a-day, one-on-one sessions trying to bring him up to speed. Still, nobody thought it would happen this fast.

Amazing?

Players just don't cross that line (of scrimmage) too often. Or that quickly. Or do it so well.

"It's huge," cornerback Jimmy Hitchcock said. "It's amazing to me that he'd come out and do so well. We can't overplay it, because it's just one game. He did a great job, but now he has to do it again.." Having said that, Hitchcock said he feels Tate is a natural corner.

"His feet are great," Hitchcock said. "His hips are just amazing. Explosive, quick, being able to turn your hips side to side. He's got the tools, no doubt about it."

And the attitude.

"People joke with Robert Tate," nose tackle Jerry Ball said. "But, in terms of heart, his heart is as big as anybody's on this team. The way he approached it, it enabled him to make the transition quicker than others, because he has that competitiveness, that "I don't want you to catch anything' attitude. A lot of the guys were coming in after the game saying, "Great game, great game." But I wasn't surprised, because I watched him work last week, to the point where I placed 100 dollars on him that he would shut Randy Moss off in practice."

Whether he did or not is unclear, but you get the point. Tate wasn't afraid and neither were the Vikings. Indeed, some people were saying that, upon reflection, Tate might have been miscast in the past. Maybe defense was always his destiny.

Astounding?

"He has confidence," Hitchcock said. "That's not a problem. I could see it growing in his face (during the game). And I grew confident in him."

But, as Hitchcock said, we'll know more about his future as a cornerback by how he responds the first time he gets beat. It didn't happen Monday, but it happens to every corner.

"I know they're going to come at me," Tate said. "Any offensive coordinator is going to say, 'I've got to go at that guy.' So I know it's going to come. And I'm going to be ready for it."

I went on to play cornerback in our final two winning games of the season against the New York Giants 34-17 and the Detroit Lions 24-17 plus a winning wildcard playoff game against the Dallas Cowboys 27-10. We lost our NFC Divisional Playoff Game against the St. Louis Rams 37-49.

The Interview

During a visit home at the end of the 1999 football season, I was interviewed by Ron Minard of **Harrisburg Magazine**. When this interview took place, I had been in the NFL as a Minnesota Viking for three years.

Below is my interview in its entirety with **Harrisburg Magazine** - *Simply the Best* edition:

Earlier this year, Robert Tate – who was Mr. Everything in his days as an athlete at Harrisburg High School – signed a new contract with the Minnesota Vikings for something in the neighborhood of the $250,000 range . . . maybe a little more, maybe a little less. He's not being specific. In any event, it's been quite a summer for the 27-year-old who's been at the pro game for just three years.

"It's hard work, but it's also play," Tate said, adding, "I've been blessed in that in my time in athletics. I've had no major injuries, none that have threatened my career anyway." As a result of that, he adds, his body "feels pretty good' and he sees no reason why he can't play another 10 years or so.

"I look at my teammates, guys who are in their late 30s and who've taken care of themselves," he continues, "and I think, Hey, I can do that," Tate, who takes pride in training hard, practicing hard and playing hard, says fitness is a way of life. "If you don't take care of yourself, you just won't last in pro sports. What we do is very difficult and what you see on Sunday is only a small part of what we go through during a season. That's the glamour part. The rest of it isn't so pretty.

During the season, Tate's day starts at 6am and rarely ends before 5pm. "I always look at it as Monday through Friday being work and then, come Sunday, it's fun" Tate says. "Once you've prepared all week long, Sunday's a time to go have some fun."

The tale end of last season was particularly fun for Tate, who had spent most of his time playing a wide receiver behind three of the more gifted wide receivers in the game. To get playing time, Tate switched to defensive halfback and spent the later part of last season adapting to that position, a position he took to like a duck in water.

When he's away from the field, the light of his life is Shekia, his 7-year-old daughter, who spends time with him in Minnesota. "I'm separated from Shekia's mom and have moved on with my life, but she and I went through a lot together and I have nothing but respect for her. It just didn't work out for us and there are times that it makes me sad."

Tate's father died eight years ago and so he spends as much time as possible in Harrisburg, where he still lives with his mom when he's in town. "My dad was there for me and my mom was there for me. It's a great family and I feel fortunate to have grown up in that environment of caring."

Former Harrisburg High School Athletic Director, Fred Clark, also comes in for words of praise from Tate. "Mr. Clark was there for me, through good times and bad. And what he did with me, how he helped me, was just what he did for all the kids. I still look up to him and respect him for the things he did for me long before I became the man I am today."

Earlier this year, **Harrisburg Magazine** Editor, Ron Minard, sat with Tate. Here is his report:

If you ever have doubts about the fact there are good young guys out there, spend a little time with Robert Tate. You will walk away reassured that whatever it is that our generation fouled up, and it was plenty, some would say, young guys like Robert Tate can make it right.

You won't find a friendlier, easier-going guy than Tate. That a 27-year-old can experience the success Tate has had and remain true to the things he learned growing up around the house 15 or 20 years ago, is a tribute to many people.

It would seem being someone like Tate in a town the size of Harrisburg would make him something a little special. He sees himself as just a regular guy. Truth is, he's anything but.

Q&A: Harrisburg's pro footballer "Robert Tate" on life in the NFL

Harrisburg Magazine: What's it like being Robert Tate?

Tate: Being Robert Tate is lots of fun. I believe waking up every day is a blessing. It means going out there on that football field every day and competing against the best there is around. I've always looked at life as a series of hurdles to clear and I always try to keep looking straight ahead and not get knocked off my stride. I don't see myself as the star that other people sometimes see. I do see myself as a role model for the kids coming up and I try to act accordingly.

HM: Do you have a nickname? How'd you get it?

Tate: My teammates call me "The Quilt' because I cover guys up and they also call me "Top Five" because I'm one of the best dressers on the team. I take pride in how I look and I always try to look my best. The guys also call me "Turbo" because I'm among the faster guys on the team, with Randy Moss. In Harrisburg, I always was called "Pint" because when I was a little baby, they could hold me in one hand. Even when I started growing, the name "Pint" stuck.

HM: Are you more comfortable in public or private?

Tate: It doesn't really matter to me if I'm in public or by myself because I always to do the right thing, to always be myself. I'm the same guy. What I do in public, I do in private. There's no difference. The way you see me is my everyday life.

HM: What's it like in Minnesota vs. Harrisburg?

Tate: People always say the big difference is that Minnesota is so cold, but I don't think it's much different from here. It may stay colder a little longer, but that's about it. There's the obvious size difference, just look at the airports and stuff. There's more to do there than here. Minnesota is a nice place to live and raise a family. Where sports are concerned, it's a great area. The people know the game; we've had three seasons of sellout crowds and the next three already are sold out. The people live and die with their football and basketball and hockey. They come and tailgate and everything. They take sports very seriously.

HM: How are you with autographs?

Tate: I'm cool with autographs. The fans here and in Minnesota and wherever I've played, have provided me with great support, and I think the autograph thing is the least I can give back. There are times you're tired of it – you've been doing it for three hours or so – and the fans don't always realize that. Still, I think signing autographs is just part of what I do, and I try to do it cheerfully. Especially here in town, a town that has been so good to me.

HM: How do you relax?

Tate: We usually play at noon on Sundays and after the games I'll grab something to eat and go home and watch the other games that are on TV.

HM: When you watch a football game on TV, what do you watch?

Tate: Because I play offense and defense, I watch both sides of the football. When I was mostly a wide receiver, I'd watch the other wide receivers, find out their likes and dislikes, try to incorporate some of what they do into my game. Toward the end of last season, I was switched to the defensive backfield, and then I had to watch what the DBs were doing.

HM: You are known for your on-the-field sense . . . for anticipating what's going to happen next. How do you do that?

Tate: It's difficult to say exactly how I play because I play so much off instinct. I did it in basketball, and I do the same in football. It's just a sense for the game that I have; I find I just do what comes naturally or automatically. I also do a lot of studying, and I think if you do your homework, if you study situations you're likely to face and those situations pop up in front of you, you simply react. And you have to react that way because that guy coming toward you can cover 40 yards in 40 seconds, and he isn't going to stop until you figure out what you're going to do. He's by you!

HM: Can you line up opposite a guy, look him in the eye and tell whether you can beat him?

Tate: Definitely. But he can do the same thing to you. Anytime I look a guy in the eye and his eyes are looking somewhere else, I'm saying, "OK! I've got you." It's the same in any sport, not just football. If I look at a guy and he's looking at the ground, I say, "OK, pal, you're in for a long, long afternoon." And it usually works out that way. I can usually tell right away if the guy I'm playing against is up for the game or not. If he's not, I'm going to give him a rough afternoon.

HM: How often do you have those long afternoons?

Tate: It's rare. The first time I switched from offense to defense, I thought it might be difficult, but it didn't turn out that way. You have to understand that I study and I prepare. When the game starts, I'm ready. If someone is going to get the best of me, he's going to have to have work very hard.

HM: Not many players in pro football – since the "60s. Anyway – have played both sides of the ball. Could you be an All-Pro on both sides of the line? Is such a thing possible?

111

Tate: Deep down, I believe I could be an All Pro, either on offense or defense. At Minnesota, we had so many quality offensive receivers that I just didn't get the chance. I was behind three of the best receivers – Randy Moss, Jake Reed, and Cris Carter – and I never had a chance to prove myself to myself or anyone else.

HM: What do you do after you make a mistake? What goes through your mind?

Tate: How I react to making a mistake depends on the situation. No matter the situation, I always try to keep my head up. Especially on defense, you have to keep your head up because that guy who just beat you may come right back on the next play and try to do it, again. When I play defensive back and I get beat, that's a touchdown. You just can't let that happen. When you're a wide receiver, you can mess up a play or two, but even then, if you do, you find yourself either on the bench or not having your number called. You just can't take a play off.

HM: Which do you like better . . . offense or defense?

Tate: I like offense best because I've played it all my life. I do think playing on defense may be my best move right now because of the opportunity it has presented me.

HM: When you're a cornerback, do you actually know what the receiver coming toward you is thinking?

Tate: I don't always know what my opponent is thinking, but I can tell, based on how he lines up and so forth, what it is he can do. If he's lined up two yards outside the number, it's either a run play or he has two pass routes he can run . . . he can do a takeoff route down the field or he's going to go 10 or 15 yards down the field and turn toward the middle. That's what he can do. And I know it.

HM: What would you do if you had to cover Robert Tate?

Tate: If I were defending Robert Tate, I would have my hands all over him. I'd be pushing and shoving. If not, it's just a track meet all day long and Robert Tate is going to give you one long afternoon that you will want to forget right away.

HM: Which is the bigger thrill . . . scoring a touchdown or smacking a wide receiver as he's just about to catch the ball?

Tate: Scoring a touchdown is more fun than smacking somebody. Offense gets all the glory and defense just does the dirty work that people really don't see.

HM: How about racism? How much of it do you see sports? In life? Are you sheltered from it?

113

Tate: Race as an issue that doesn't get much of my attention. I can talk to a person and listen to them and I know where they stand and how we can relate to each other. People who aren't tolerant and understanding just don't get much of my time . . . and that goes not only for on the football field, but also in society as a whole.

HM: How about jealousy among high-paid athletes?

Tate: I think jealousy among athletes is hidden, but I believe there is plenty of it because we are competing for jobs and for salaries. If someone has taken your spot on the team, you want it back. Think about it; if you want a job; you have to take it from a teammate, someone you sit in meetings with, someone you travel with, someone you share your life with. But you have to compete with them. Jealousies develop, but it's only human.

HM: What kind of money do players such as yourself make . . . never mind what gets reported.

Tate: Wide Receivers probably make about $200,000 to $300,000. As you know, taxes take a lot of it and it's not like most people think. At the end, there's not always that much left for most guys . . . not the superstars, but for most of the guys, it's really not all that much. I can understand why some people think it's a lot of money but you have to remember that it's a whole different lifestyle

114

than what most people experience. It goes fast if you don't budget your money and take care of it. There always are others trying to get a piece of it.

HM: What kind of a car do you drive?
Tate: I have a 1998 Ford Expedition

HM: How much do you worry about being injured? How do you deal with that?
Tate: I try not to think about getting hurt because when you realize any play could be your last play - and you focus on that – that's when something happens. I just go out there in practice and in the game and play hard. If something happens, at least I will know I played hard, and I didn't get injured because I was going half speed or something.

HM: What kind of things make you laugh?
Tate: I don't know if laugh is the word, but what makes me smile is the fact I have the opportunity to play professional football. And my daughter makes me smile. She's a sweetheart.

HM: Who's the most famous person you've met?
Tate: I'd say Michael Jordan is the most famous person I've met so far. He is friends with Randy Moss, my teammate, and Randy introduced us in Chicago.

115

HM: When was the last time you were alone?

Tate: At night, I'm always alone. I like to be by myself. I don't like to party; I don't run around or drink or go out. I may stop in some place, but I'm right back out. I don't stick around.

HM: How much do you party?

Tate: I don't party. I have my cousin, Ronny Daniels, and he's the only one I really hang out with. There was Donnie Weaver who was my role model when I was playing here. He stuck with me through thick and thin and was always there for me, helping me out. When it comes to partying, I try to be seen – I grew up here; I have friends here and I don't want them to think I've gotten too big or stuff like that – but I really don't party all that much. I'm not a Lexus and Rolex guy. Once you see me do that, you'll know something's wrong with Robert Tate. It just isn't me.

HM: How much do you believe in luck? You know, Deion Sanders had his lucky shorts, the green ones with the white dollar signs all over them. Do you have any little things you do . . . superstitions?

Tate: I believe in luck sometimes . . . a ball bounces off your head and you turn around and catch it. That's luck. I am superstitious. I have to have my socks right. My left shoe goes on first. I did that in high school. I have my game-day routine way of getting dressed, the way I look when I go on the field. If I don't do these things, I'm inclined to believe I will have a bad game. Yes, I'm superstitious.

HM: What do you want to do when your career is over?

Tate: I want to stay in sports . . . maybe in coaching in either football or basketball. I wouldn't mind coaching. I love kids and I would enjoy coaching at the high school level and maybe moving up. I relate well to kids and can motivate them, tell them how life really is, especially in sports, but also just in general. I would like leading kids in the right direction.

HM: You know the picture of pro athletes . . . women in every town. The good life on the road. etc. How much of that is fact? How much of it is fiction?

Tate: I'd say it's 50-50. When you're in the limelight, when you're making the money, there will be women out there. And there will be others who aren't really trying to be your friend. For me, it's a matter of trusting those who have been there for me along the way. Right now, my daughter's mother - I'm not with her - has been with me through thick and thin, when I didn't have a thing. It didn't work out for us and I've moved on with my life, but she and I share and understand because we were together for so much. I respect her.

117

HM: With most athletes, the really good ones, anyway, you'll hear them talking about sometimes being in a "zone." Michael Jordan used to talk about the times in a game when he just knew everything he shot would go in. Have you ever found that zone? Where everything you touch or think, works? If so, what's it like?

Tate: I've had games when it was like that. I can remember even back to playing basketball at Harrisburg High when I'd be like that . . . it would seem like the basket was as big as the ocean and all you had to do was throw the ball and it would go in. Football's the same. I've had games when I was catching the ball, when I had the guy defending me on his heels. In those situations, I wanted the ball thrown to me every play . . . I just knew I was going to catch it. When I played defensive back last year, there were times when I was knocking down all the balls, knocking the receiver down and I'd say "come on, come on. Come my way again." I was just ready to go.

HM: How do you get in that zone? How does it happen?

Tate: I don't have a clue. It's just there are times when it's just there. It's like a light bulb goes on and you know you're in that zone. You just feel that whatever it is that needs doing, you can do it. You just can't miss.

HM: How about some guys you don't want to play against because they're so good, so tough?

Tate: It's more true on offense that I'd look up and see guys I didn't want to run against. Usually, it would be certain linebackers . . . like Junior Sean. When I'd look up and see him there, I'd think. "Wow! This is going to be a game." And you'd want to bring your "A" game on those days. I never worried too much about defensive backs. They might hit you, but they can't hurt you. Linebackers, they're different.

HM: Can football make you rich?

Tate: It can and it can't. Where I am right now, it can't make me rich. There are guys who make millions of dollars. I'm not one of them at this point. And even those guys who make the money have to know how to handle it. I think I know how to handle it but not everyone does. Once you have the money, there are always people who want it because they think it will make them happy. Well, it's not my job to give the money, to make them happy.

HM: Does it matter to you who coaches your team?

Tate: It really doesn't matter too much who coaches. It doesn't really matter who my teammates are, either. All I want to be able to do is look them in the eye and know that they're willing to go to war with me because

119

that's what we do each game . . . we go to war. If the guy next to me is ready to do that, I don't care who he is.

HM: What's the best feature of your game?

Tate: I think my willingness to practice at 110 percent every day is my best feature because I believe how you practice is how you play. You can't turn it on and off. I believe that.

HM: Growing up in Harrisburg, how did you stay out of trouble? Did you stay out of trouble?

Tate: I had one incident in high school where they said I threw a book at a teacher and that was about it for me. I can tell you today, I didn't throw the book but that is an incident that has stayed with me and I am truly sorry about it. But beyond that, I was a pretty normal kid.

HM: What about peer pressure? What would you tell today's high school kids?

Tate: I'd tell today's kids that there will always be peer pressure but that you don't have to go along with the gang, with the rest of the kids. I feel pressure even today but it's in selecting an agent, deciding how much money my talent is worth, sorting out the kinds of people I want to run with, that kind of stuff. As for the kids, I think if they're hanging out with other kids who are doing things they

120

don't want to do – drinking or drugs or whatever – it's up to the individual guy to say, "Hey, I'm not doing that. I'm outta here." It's never easy, but you feel better when you stand up for what you believe is right, for what you've been taught is right. I think when you walk away, you win, and you're being smart.

HM: Where are your childhood pals today? Any of em dead?

Tate: My childhood friends are still around, still going strong. I still enjoy them and we keep in touch. One or two of those guys I grew up with may have passed away, but almost all of them are still around. We're still friends.

HM: Three last questions: First, what will you miss most about football?

Tate: The thing I'd miss most about football would be the competition. I never go through the motions, I compete. Every day. In practice, in the game. I would miss the competition.

HM: Second, how difficult will it be for you to walk away?

Tate: It will be very difficult. It's all I've ever done, and I love it. Walking away will be very difficult for me.

HM: Do you think Wilt Chamberlain lied when he claimed to have had sex with 20,000 women?

Tate: From everything I've heard – and when a guy has that kind of money, there are lots of women hanging around, that's for sure – I wouldn't say it was out of the question.

The end of the interview

Starting Cornerback

In November 2000, I replaced veteran cornerback Jimmy Hitchcock and became the Vikings starting right cornerback! My number was also changed from 81 to a 28. I got a lot of playing time when I successfully switched to cornerback. I was no longer hidden beneath wide receivers, Chris Carter, Jake Reed and Randy Moss. I was my own man now as a cornerback and I was enjoying it.

My First Interception

The next Sunday, I made my first interception of the season against the Carolina Panthers! That was an awesome feeling! I had a feeling all day that something special was going to happen in this game and it sure did. I also led the Vikings with ten tackles in this game. We went on to win the game 31-17.

I finally knew I had made a successful transition to cornerback when one day as I ran out of the tunnel with the team and trotted onto the metrodome turf when I heard the fans begin to call my name! It felt so good. Ever since I became a Viking, I had always dreamed of that happening, and it finally did. I was now a bona fide cornerback and it felt great!

Dating Again

By this time I had met and began dating a young lady named Sheree Pederson from Minnesota. She would come to most of our home games and we became closer and closer and soon developed a great relationship with each other.

Over the next several years we had two children together; a daughter named Arriana and a son named Robert, III. Sheree also had a son named Stephon from a previous relationship.

I can still remember when I first brought Sheree to Harrisburg to officially meet my mom, Thomas and my brother and sisters. Everyone hit it off very well. My parents welcomed Sheree to the family.

Six months later, I proposed to Sheree and she said, "Yes!"

Moving On Up

By now I was making a lot more money and I finally moved out of my one bedroom apartment in Eden Prairie and into a brand new home. This was an extremely big move for me and I made this move with my fiancé Sheree and our children. Our four-bedroom, four-bathroom house in Shakopee, had an open spiral staircase off the living room. It had a completely finished three-room basement with wall to wall carpeting where I had a game room that housed my pool table and pin ball machine; a large family room; a bathroom with a Jacuzzi and a guest bedroom. In the backyard our deck led to our pool. I also had a basketball court area set up in the backyard and a children's playground for the kids. We had a three-car garage that housed my Yukon Denali, my motor bike and Sheree's Chevy Tahoe. There was plenty of room for my oldest daughter Shekia to stay when she flew up from Harrisburg for visits with me. Also, when my parents flew up to visit me again, they would not have to stay in a hotel anymore.

Back in Harrisburg, my parents moved too. They moved out of the city into a four-bedroom, two bath split level home in the suburbs of Susquehanna Township. Their house has an open country floor plan, a large family room in the lower level, a pool in the backyard and a two-car garage to house my mom's seven-passenger Ford Windstar mini van and Thomas's Pontiac Grand Am. I always liked to see my mom smile, and she was smiling big when she moved into her new home.

I kept trying to get my mom to move to Minnesota, but she always said it was too cold. She did not have a problem with coming to visit me, but she said moving to Minnesota was out of the question.

In the meantime, I was taking to my new position as cornerback like a fish takes to water. I was having fun with it and I was getting the job done!

In the Vikings Update, in the Extra Points section, staff writer Tony Parker wrote: "Minnesota's Defensive Coordinator Emmitt Thomas said, 'Right now, Robert Tate is way ahead of the schedule. He plays as well as a lot of corners who played their whole career in college and possibly in the pros right now. He knows how to finish plays and he works hard, and that's what separates him from being just an average or normal corner.' Tate's raw talent and work ethic were key to his transition to cornerback."

What helped me a lot was an understanding of the receiver's routes. You can't go out there just guessing routes. If you do, they'll pump it and go up on you. But having a feel for offensive formations and sets, plus having been on the other side, it helped me go to the ball once it was in the air.

In a 2000 season opening game against the Chicago Bears, the Bears found that the only way to keep me away from the ball was to run at me. However, the Vikings had a 30-27 victory and I played a critical part to that win. I was in on four crucial tackles and I did not let a receiver get behind me. My timing throughout the game was on the money. After the game, reporters waited for the opportunity to interview me. They spotted me leaving the building. A reporter for a local television station asked me for an interview. I promptly obliged. The next week, in the Vikings 13-7 victory over the Miami Dolphins, I made three tackles. In that game, I also knocked a ball away from Miami's Tony Martin.

Monday Night Football – October 9, 2000 - Tampa Bay vs Vikings – Star Tribune Staff Writer, Kent Youngblood wrote, "On the game's second play from scrimmage, Tampa Bay Wide Receiver, Keyshawn Johnson, lost the ball after a hit by cornerback Tate. The Vikings recovered the ball and scored on the next play. The Minnesota Vikings took advantage of two more Tampa Bay fumbles to take a 20-16 lead after three quarters. The Vikings went on to win the game 30-23.'

Vikings vs Buffalo Bills – Sunday, October 22, 2009. The Vikings scored their second touchdown in the second quarter after Aaron Stecker's fumbled kickoff return. In the fourth quarter, Tate was able to throw the knockout blow. Quarterback Flutie hit Price for what was supposed to be a first down, but Tate hit Price hard, forcing him to fumble."

I was just trying to make sure that I brought him down. But I hit him high. If it's a bigger guy, I would have hit lower, but

I went up top with the ball, and fortunately, the ball came out. Vikings won 31-27.

Summer Training Camp

When our week-long training camp started the first week of August 2001, temperatures at the Vikings training camp in Mankato, Minnesota were in the 90s and the humidity made it feel like 120 degrees! I kept drinking water so I would not get dehydrated, but it did not seem like it was enough. Practicing in this heat was stifling. A heat advisory had been issued from the National Weather Services for the area. But the team still practiced. My teammate All-Pro defensive tackle Corey Stringer seemed to be having a little problem with the heat on the first day of camp. I was even having a hard time dealing with this intense heat, but somehow we all made it through that first day of camp.

The next day I showed up at camp to another day of scorching hot heat. We were pushing ourselves to the point of exhaustion in that hot humid heat. The coaches made sure that we took plenty of water breaks during practice. We continued to practice and run our drills with the sweat dripping off of us. All of a sudden, Corey Stringer collapsed. He was rushed to the hospital but Stringer died early the next morning, due to complications from heatstroke. He was only 27 years old. That was a very traumatic time for the entire Viking team, coaches included. Stringer's death caused the NFL to review training camp practices. We were all saddened by the loss of Corey. That year we fell to a dismal 5-11 season.

One of the worst losses for me as a Viking, was in the NFC Championship game on a very cold day on January 14, 2001, against the New York, Giants at the Meadowlands. We were playing for the NFC title. We had a great week of practice and a great plan for the Giants. But they took away our game plan early in the game. Once they established their game plan, it got real tough for us. In that game, I intercepted QB Kerry Collins once, forced a fumble, and had six tackles. But it was to no avail. The Vikings overall just played an all-around bad football game – offense, defense and special teams. Daunte Culpepper, Randy Moss and Cris Carter couldn't get anything going. There is just no way you would think that you would go out like that and not score any points, not even a field goal. I mean, we were favored to win that game. But you have to give the Giants credit. They came out and did their homework and they studied us. Anytime you can shut out our team like that, you know you did your homework. The Giants beat us an embarrassing 41-0.

Released By The Vikings

Even though I had another good season as a cornerback for the Vikings, I was released at the end of the 2002 season.

I started all 16 regular-season games as a cornerback for the Vikings and had three interceptions over my career with the Vikings, two for a touchdown. I played in 67 games over my five-year stay in Minnesota. However, I was now a free agent.

I took Sheree and our children on a vacation to Hawaii and everyone had a wonderful time.

Later that year, I found a new home with the Baltimore Ravens.

Baltimore Ravens

I signed a one-year contract with the Ravens as a defensive back and kickoff returner in August 2002. On August 22, 2002 CBS Sports Online wrote,

"The Baltimore Ravens Pick Up Robert Tate in 2002 - 'He's a guy who has started at corner for two championship games,' Ravens Head Coach and former Minnesota coordinator Brian Billick said. What he brings us in terms experience...absolutely, in the nickel and dime packages, he's an excellent returner. He fills a lot of voids for us." Coach Billick went on to say that 'Tate will play against the Philadelphia Eagles in the Ravens' third pre-season game on Friday and could be a candidate to start once the regular season begins."

129

I can remember packing up and leaving Minnesota, my home of five years. It was kind of bittersweet because of the friendships I was leaving behind. However, I did not move alone. My fiancé Sheree and our children packed up and moved to Baltimore too.

We moved to Owings Mills, MD and after a couple weeks, we finally got settled in. We leased a house two miles from the Baltimore Ravens training facilities and three miles from the Baltimore Ravens stadium, now called the M&T Bank Stadium.

Since I lived so close to my hometown of Harrisburg, PA, I visited home quite regularly. Also, instead of flying to my home games in Baltimore, now my parents were able to drive the 90-minute ride to Baltimore to see me play.

NFL Monday Night Football is the premier prime-time televised game of all NFL teams. This is the game that all football players always get hyped about and want to do great things. You definitely do not want to fumble, miss a tackle or get sacked on Monday Night Football.

On Monday Night Football, September 30, 2002, it was the Ravens vs. Broncos. I took the second half kickoff and ran it back 64 yards to set up a field goal that made the score 34-3. The Broncos tried desperately to get back in the game and they almost did! But we won 34-23.

The next week, November 10, 2002 in our 37-27 victory over the Cincinnati Bengals, I had three tackles and a pass deflection.

But sadly, after my one-year contract ended with the Baltimore Ravens, my contract was not extended. I was once again, a free agent.

I did enjoy my one-year stay with the Baltimore Ravens as I was learning their system. I always enjoy a challenge and I believe I arose to the occasion when playing for the Ravens. I played in 13 games, had 1 pass deflection, 2 fumble recoveries, 12 tackles, 1 assist and 17 returns for 356 yards. My one-year contract with the Baltimore Ravens ended in February, 2003. I was once again, an unrestricted free agent.

Once again, my fiancé and I packed up and moved our family back to our home in Shakopee, Minnesota.

For the year that I was out of the NFL, I concentrated my efforts on running my youth football and basketball camps. I also spoke to youth at school assemblies in Minnesota and Harrisburg about the importance of receiving a quality education and setting goals for their future.

I remained a free agent for one year then found another home in the NFL.

Robert Tate

CHAPTER 10

The NFL Off-Seasons

I always came home during the NFL off-seasons. While I was home in 2000, I enjoyed the chance to spend time with my daughter, Shekia.

It always feels good to come back home to Harrisburg. I stayed with my mom and Thomas whenever I came back home.

Sometimes when I came home, people would say things to me like, "Why are you back here? You're in the NFL now; you can live anywhere you want." I just smile and tell them, "I have roots in Harrisburg; this is where I grew up; that's why I keep coming back. And as long as my daughter and my mom live in Harrisburg, I am going to keep coming back."

Young kids would walk up to me and say, "Where is your Hummer Robert Tate? Where are your body guards? Why aren't you in a limo? Do you do Cribs Robert Tate?

I tell them I don't drive around in pricey rides like a Hummer, Lamborghini, Ferrari or a Mercedes-Benz. That's just not me. But since I do like my rides, I tell them my luxury ride was a Yukon Denali Sports Utility Truck. I spend my money wisely. Some people say I am one of the cheapest guys in the NFL because I don't go on luxury vacations to exotic places or wear large expensive gold and diamond chains around my neck. They say I am too frugal with my money, but to that I say, "I know the value of a dollar."

I don't splurge on myself much, but I do splurge on my children and my mom on occasions. I sent my mom and Thomas on a five-day cruise to the Bahamas as their wedding anniversary present.

Sometimes I do splurge on myself a little bit; I just don't get crazy with it like ordering a bunch of custom made suits when suits off the rack look just as nice. Actually, I still enjoy shopping in Target and I spend a lot of time and money in Walmart. Some people just don't understand that. But even though I'm in the NFL, I'm still just your average kind of guy.

My Football and Basketball Camps

I hosted my annual Robert Tate two-day football camp at Harrisburg High School with the help of my sponsors: Giant, Subway and Mayor Stephen Reed. There were about 80 boys and girls in attendance at the camp. This football camp received a lot of local media attention. I was interviewed at camp by our local TV news and by our local Patriot News. On Channel 27 News they showed a segment of all the kids working out and having fun at

134

the camp. The kids had a lot of energy and came ready for two days of workouts. At camp, we also gave information to the athlete and their parents regarding nutrition and exercise. We teach the kids the fundamentals of football, as well as how to be a well-rounded athlete. Two weeks later, I had my annual Robert Tate Basketball Camp. The basketball camp for boys and girls was held at the Camp Curtin YMCA in uptown Harrisburg.

I also have a champion basketball team called the "Pints" that I sponsor every summer at the YMCA. The Pints play in the YMCA summer youth league each year. In 2008, the "Pints" were crowned Champion of the Little League Basketball Program! When I'm not home, my cousin Ronny Daniels is the Head Coach of the Pints basketball team.

My son Malachi was born on November 8, 2001. He was born in the Hershey Medical Center. I can already tell my little guy is going to be a great athlete one day, just by the way he held the football when he was only two years old.

Chairman of the Board

I was elected to fill the seat of Chairman of the Athletes Advisory Board for the National Alliance of African American Athletes. I replaced the Rev. Reggie White, former Linebacker for the Green Bay Packers, as Head of the Alliance. The Alliance is the oldest organization of African American athletes in the country and is dedicated to improving success rates and social responsibility for all African American athletes.

On June 28, 2002, the Inauguration was held for me at the Harrisburg Martin Luther King City Government Center. The Mistress of Ceremonies was my cousin Dolly Tate, Alpha Kappa Alpha Sorority, Inc.

I now lead the Alliance and its many-faceted efforts to improve the professional and private lives of African American athletes. The Alliance is the largest group of black athletes working together in the nation and annually conducts an array of programs and activities around the country. J. Everette Pearsall is the Executive Director of the Alliance.

Retirement of my High School Jersey # 22 – and My Elementary School Gymnasium Named After Me

In 2003, Harrisburg High retired my football jersey # 22. That was an incredibly touching moment for me. But on top of that on the same day, the Mayor renamed my elementary school gym after me! It was now called "The Robert Tate Gymnasium." I was humbled by this showing of love and support. The program read:

A Celebration and Dedication Ceremony

Commemorating the Renaming of the Steele School Gymnasium

In Honor of Robert Tate
AND
The Retirement of Number 22

Mayor Stephen R. Reed, City of Harrisburg

Tuesday, February 11, 2003

The most recognizable student-athlete to attend Steele School, Robert Tate became an All-American running back at Harrisburg high School. He rushed for over 1,000 yards three times in his high school career. He attended the University of Cincinnati for four years majoring in general studies. In 1995 he was named Conference USA offensive player of the Year and Special Teams Player of the Year. Tate's professional football career began in 1997 with the Minnesota Vikings. He entered the National Football League as a wide receiver and kickoff returner.

In 1999, he was switched to cornerback and became a starter for the heralded Minnesota Viking defense. In 2002, Tate was released by the Vikings but quickly found a new home with the Baltimore Ravens, and is a defensive back and kickoff returner.

Robert Tate has always been very active in our community. He is a volunteer at the Camp Curtin Branch YMCA. He spends time in our local schools sharing positive messages of hope to the students in the Harrisburg City School District.

Stephen R. Reed, Mayor
City of Harrisburg

Committee Members:

Dr. Gerald Kohn	Mark Pisco
Julie Botel	Kirk Smallwood
Vera Cornish	

Chapter 11

Arizona Cardinals

On February 4, 2004, I signed a one-year contract to play for the Arizona Cardinals, with Head Coach Dennis Green (my former coach from the Minnesota Vikings). My contract went on to be extended for a total of three years with the Cardinals.

My fiancé Sheree and our children had to pack up and move again, this time to the hot desert heat in Arizona. We moved about four miles from the Arizona training facility where I would eventually workout five days a week.

I came to Arizona and met with the coaching staff, and had to study a new playbook.

I did not waste any time in making my presence known in my first game against the San Francisco 49ers. On Sunday, October 2nd, I had two tackles, a pass deflection, a 22-yard interception and a forced 49er fumble! I was all over the field in this game. I guess I just wanted to prove that the Coach Green did not make a mistake in signing me to the Arizona

Cardinals organization. We won the game Cardinals 31- 49ers 14.

The next Sunday, on October 9, 2004, in a game against the Carolina Panthers, I had my second interception of the season. I ran the ball back 25 yards. I also deflected a pass and made four tackles. But in spite of quarterback Josh McCowin having a huge game with 394 yards in the air, we lost the game to the Panthers 24-20.

Marriage

As mentioned previously, Sheree and I have three children. We have a beautiful daughter named Arriana Marie Tate who was born in Minnesota and who is now eight years old and is a daddy's girl. Her birthday is May 21st. Arriana is a cheerleader, she has dance recitals and plays basketball. My handsome little guy, Robert Lee Tate, III (Trey), was also born in Minnesota and is now five-years-old. He is already an athlete playing soccer and baseball and he is really good. His birthday is March 4th. My cool stepson Stephon is now 15 and plays basketball and football and is good in both sports.

On February 14, 2005, Sheree and I got married in Las Vegas at the Luxury Venetian Resort Hotel in the Bellagio Chapel. Our children were all a part of our wedding ceremony, including my oldest daughter Shekia as a junior bridesmaid. My youngest daughter

Arriana was a flower girl, my son Trey was ring bearer and my stepson Stephon was a junior usher along with my little brother Spencer.

Our wedding reception was held in the Grand Venetian Ballroom. My mom and Thomas and about 70 family members and friends were in attendance.

Living in Arizona

The climate from Minnesota and Arizona are as different as night and day. It is hot with dry heat in Arizona and the rainfall is scarce. I had to get used to seeing very little green grass. But once I got used to the climate in Arizona, I decided to make it my home. So Sheree and I sold our home in Minnesota and I purchased a home in Chandler, Arizona. I tried to get my mom to move to Arizona but she said she did not like the dry-heat hot climate on a permanent basis. (I secretly think my mom is set in her ways and just doesn't want to leave Harrisburg). But it's okay.

One year my mom, Thomas, my brother and sisters and daughter Shekia all flew to Arizona to spend Easter with us. It was great having all my family together. We all went to church on Easter Sunday which was really nice. Sheree and I had invited a couple friends with their kids over for Easter dinner. Sheree and my mom prepared the meal and everything was delicious! Our guests brought some tasty deserts which we ate after dinner. After dessert, I had an Easter Egg Hunt in my front yard for the kids. They had a great time running around finding the Easter eggs. Along with the real dyed eggs, we also hid a lot of colorful plastic eggs that had money in them. We gave a prize to the one who found the most money. We hid about 100 eggs and there were about 15 children. They were scrambling all over the place finding those eggs. After the Easter hunt was over, they all played in the Big Bouncy Jump, Dunk, Climb and Slide inflatable that I had rented for the day. It was set up in my front yard and the kids all enjoyed jumping up and down in it and sliding down the slide. The parents just sat out in lounge chairs sipping on cool drinks, enjoying each other's company as we watched our children having a great time. That was one of the best Easter's that I had in a very long time.

Cardinals Football

In the three years I was a Cardinal, we never made it to the playoffs. We started out slow this year too but we were still hoping to make it to the playoffs.

It was three years in the making but we finally got a new football stadium in August of 2006. Our new stadium, named the University of Phoenix Stadium is located in Glendale, AZ.

We were very excited to be playing the Chicago Bears in our new stadium on Monday Night Football, October 16, 2006. The Bears were unbeaten at 5-0 which was their best start in two decades. The Cardinals were 1-4. We desperately NEEDED to win this game.

The energy level was high, mom and Thomas were there, the fans showed up in full force and we were ready to play football. The whole team was psyched up for this game. It seemed like the whole state of Arizona got caught up in the excitement.

Even though All-Pro wide receiver Larry Fitzgerald was injured and couldn't play in the game, we still had veteran Anquan Boldin and newly acquired veteran running back, Edgerrin James. In the first quarter, our quarterback Matt Leinert threw for two first quarter touchdowns. We were winning 20-0 at halftime. But the second half was a little different; we let the Bears get on the scoreboard. With five minutes left in the 4th quarter, we were now only winning by six points with a score at Cardinals 23 – Bears 17. To make a long story short, Rackers missed a late field goal attempt and we ended up losing to the Bears 24-23. That was an embarrassing and heartbreaking loss. Even though we all had to take the blame in blowing a 20-point advantage, that loss was a bitter pill to swallow. The Bears went on to win the Super Bowl against the New York Giants that year.

I was re-signed again for another year with the Cardinals in October 2006. When I returned to the lineup for my third year, my first game was against the 49ers. In that game I had two tackles, a pass deflection, an interception and a forced fumble. I had a very busy day that day.

Visiting Sick Children

During the regular football season, the Cardinal football players would visit hospitals to read to children. I went with our team mascot, Big Red, to read to a group of children in Banner Children's Hospital in Mesa, AZ. Since I had young children, I borrowed some books from them to read to the pediatric patients. I let my children pick out several books that they thought would be good for me to read to the children in the hospital. I think the kids really enjoyed the stories I read because they had smiles on their faces. I also gave stuffed animals for the group of kids I read to. I thought that if I brought in some stuffed animals, it could bring some lightness to their hearts. Anytime you are a part of a NFL organization and anytime you have the opportunity to come out and do stuff like this, it is a blessing to me. That is the way I grew up and I wish I could do stuff like this all of the time. Especially after you look at some of the circumstances these kids have gone through.

In my third year with the Arizona Cardinals, I played my final game on December 31st against the San Diego Chargers. We lost that game by a touchdown. The score was Charges 27 - Cardinals 20.

After sitting out one year, I officially retired from the NFL in 2008.

Chapter 12

Coach Dennis Green

Some people in Harrisburg used to say that I was chosen in the NFL Draft because of my ties to Coach Dennis Green and that he would take care of me. That was not true because I never knew Coach Green in Harrisburg. I found out after I was drafted by the Vikings that Coach Green attended the same high school as me, Harrisburg High (formerly John Harris High School) and was also a star running back on the football team, just like I was which I thought was neat. However, Coach Green attended high school 25 years previous to me attending.

My mom said she never knew Coach Green until I became a Minnesota Viking. So as far as Coach Green taking care of me, that is just not true and never has been true. In fact, if the New York Jets had received their pick before the Vikings, I would have been selected by the Jets. During the draft, Coach Parcels had already called my house and told me he was going to pick me with their next selection and for me to wait by the phone for their phone call. But the Vikings picked before the Jets and Coach Green selected me.

Even though I was a wide receiver in college, when I was drafted by the Vikings, Coach Green drafted me because of my kick-off return and punt return skills. Since I was number one in the nation in kickoff returns in college and they needed another specialist for the Vikings, my name was called to fill that spot. If Coach Green was recruiting players from his high school Alma Mater, he could have also chosen other high school alumni such as Kenny Watson or Hank Poteat in other NFL Drafts. But he chose me to fill a need that the Vikings had and there was nothing personal about it.

The NFL is a business that is based on inches, wins and losses. If you can't cut the cake then you will be cut. It's just as simple as that. If you can't produce, then you just will not be on the roster long. If you get injured, you can't help the team win games, so again, you will not be on a NFL roster long. If your team is losing too many games, the team owners need to find a fix. They either make the decision to get rid of some players or else the coach will lose their jobs. In Minnesota, Coach Green was a great coach. Every year he had more wins than losses. He got the Vikings to the playoffs every year, even to a Championship game. But there were complaints that he could not make it to the big game, the Super Bowl. Even though Coach

Green had friendships with the Vikings ownership team, that still did not stop him from being fired from the Vikings franchise in 2002, one year before his contract expired. Mr. Red McCombs, the Vikings owner bought out the final year of his contract. In the NFL, it is all about winning.

My Personal Feelings about Dennis Green

Even though I had never met Coach Green prior to him selecting me in the NFL Draft, he was like a father figure to me over the eight seasons we spent together. We spent five years together in Minnesota as a Viking and three years together as an Arizona Cardinal. I could talk to Coach Green about football, about relationships and about the business of being a professional athlete. I could talk to him just like I could always talk to my dad. In some ways, my dad and Coach Green were alike. Coach Green even had the same body language of disappointment that my dad had, that stern look, that crossing of the arms and that raised eyebrow. Those expressions said it all for me. I never wanted to let my father down and now I did not want to let Coach Green down. After all, he gave me the opportunity to become a professional football player by drafting me out of the University of Cincinnati. (I know my dad was smiling big time up in heaven on this day as he was telling everyone, "That's my boy!")

Robert Tate

Coach Green knew when to turn on the emotion, when to keep it loose and when to let you have it. In my opinion, Coach Green was and is still hands down, the best coach in the National Football League. I would go to war for Coach Green anytime. After all, he helped to make my dream of playing in the NFL come true.

PART FIVE

Robert Tate

Chapter 13

Commentary about the Game

The average career of a NFL player is only 2.5 years. Some careers are considerably longer and some careers are considerably shorter. But the average career is 2.5 years. I feel blessed to have been a part of the NFL for nine years, which was well above average, and to come away from the game without any injuries is a true blessing.

The average football player's career is so short because of the brutal nature of the sport. Running backs get hit repeatedly in every game they play. Sometimes they get hit so hard by a linebacker it feels like your head is about to fall off. The quarterback also takes a lot of punishment when the defense gets past the linemen who are supposed to protect him. Every defense player is always trying to get credit for that quarterback sack. The wide receivers also have a vulnerable position; especially when the quarterback throws the ball high and the wide receiver has to jump up to catch it. The moment their feet leave the ground, they are in an exposed position to receive a serious injury. Getting hit while in the air poses a great risk for injury. A lot of wide receivers will not put themselves out there like that to catch a high ball, because of the potential of serious injury.

My teammate for the Vikings, premier running back Robert Smith, retired at the top of his game after breaking the Vikings' franchise rushing record by running for 1,521 yards in 2000. Nobody knew but Robert what punishment his body had endured prior to his abrupt retirement at the age of 28.

Football for me has always been and still is a fun and competitive sport. I have played this sport most of my life, but I also know you can get seriously injured. Actually, you are always only one game away from an injury. You can receive a career-ending injury at any given time and never be able to play the game again. But you cannot focus on getting hurt. If you do, that is when something will happen. Many players constantly play with pain from one week to the next. They come in the game taped up, wrapped up, shot up with pain-killer drugs ready to play the game. They do whatever it takes to play 60-minutes of football.

In the game, a player can twist their ankle when making a cut to the sidelines that can put him out of commission or he can get tackled so hard they end up with a torn ligament, which can be very painful. Constantly getting hit takes it toll on your body, no matter if your body is in great condition or not.

Helmet-to-helmet hits can cause serious damage. Since this type of hit is so dangerous, seven safety regulations have been implemented by the NFL. You can get a concussion or worse, get brain damage that can have deadly consequences from helmet-to-helmet hits. But in spite of the roughness of the game, and the potential injury in the game, I still enjoyed the competitiveness of the sport.

I have learned from my nine years in the NFL that this sport is not for the meek or the weak. This is a game of strength, muscle and power. There are many players who try to get inside your head by talking smack to you on the line and taunting you. They talk about your mama, your girlfriend, they even challenge your manhood. They say anything to get under your skin to make you make a mistake. When you do, they are all over you.

For me, I practiced hard and I played hard and I never second-guessed myself. If I ever sustained an injury, it was not going to because I tried to shield myself; it was going to be because I was in it to win it. All NFL athletes really have to keep their body conditioned in order to be effective in the game. Even in the off-season, you still have to work out to keep your body in tip-top shape. But if you do not like getting hit, the NFL is not for you.

I cannot stress enough that the NFL is a hard-hitting sport and you can become severely injured in the game. I personally think a pro athlete deserves every penny of their high salaries because of the brutal nature of the sport, the risks a player takes with their bodies and the pain they have to endure in order to compete in the game on Sundays.

NFL players need to stay in shape during the football season and continue to work out during the NFL off-season. Being a professional football player is a full-time job. Players who become the dominate player of any sport are the players who work hardest during the off season to stay in shape and master their skills. Just like everything else in life, people who work the hardest to master their trade, are the same people who are the most successful in their line of work. In football, we have to constantly work out to keep our body conditioned and in good shape. If you don't, you will not last long in professional football.

I had a strength and conditioning coach that I worked with four times a week when I was in the NFL. The NFL training facilities have state-of-the-art training equipment which was available seven days a week. Working out is second nature to me now because I've been doing it for so long. Even though I do not play football any longer, I still continue to work out at least four times a week. I won't feel right if I don't work out.

Your teammates in the NFL become one big family. The player wives, girlfriends and kids get to know each other and some form a bond with each other. They usually sit with each other on game day. NFL players are allowed family passes for their family for every home game. The passes allow the player families to be in the NFL Family Room before and after the games enjoying a full hot and cold buffet meal provided free of charge. There is also an open bar with no charge. There are TVs throughout the Family Room so you can watch the football games. All of this is free as long as you have a family pass. The Family Room is closed when the 1st quarter of the game begins.

When the game is over, the Family Room is opened again. Your family can wait for you in the comfort of the Family Room while enjoying refreshments and snacks. Since it takes a little time for the players to get showered, dressed and sometimes interviewed, family members can wait in the comfort of the Family Room until the players come out. We meet our families in the Family Room and walk out of the building to an area that is secured by security guards and is roped off with a pathway for us to walk to our cars in the NFL player parking lot. There are always a lot of fans on either side of the ropes asking and sometimes even begging for an autograph.

You acquire lasting friendships with many of your teammates. At the University of Cincinnati, I played alongside Sam Garnes who was drafted in the 1997 NFL draft with me and Chris Hewett and Anthony Ladd who made NFL rosters as free agents. In Minnesota, I played alongside great players like Cris Carter, Randy Moss, Robert Griffith and Daunte Culpepper.

In Baltimore, I enjoyed my experience playing alongside great players such as Ray Lewis, Jamal Lewis, and Jeff Blake. In Arizona, I played alongside great players like Larry Fitzgerald, Anquan Boldin, and Kurt Warner. I still have friendships with most of these players today.

My experience as an athlete with a job playing football in the NFL is an experience I will remember for the rest of my life. I have enjoyed playing sports all my life, and in the NFL, I got paid to do what I loved to do. I gave it my all in every game and on every play because of my love of the sport.

In spite of all the obstacles that got in my way, I continued to focus and my childhood dream came true.

Chapter 14

Reflections

Parenting My Children

As a parent, sometimes you need to be a little stern with your children, while other times a hug and a kiss will do. As a parent, you also need to know the difference; meaning you need to know when a hug is in order, being stern is in order or tough love is required.

I've certainly made my share of mistakes with my children over the years. Maybe I have punished one of my children a little too harshly or yelled at them without cause or sometimes, maybe I was a little too easy. But I have learned through my mistakes that yelling at my children is not the best way to teach them.

Maybe I have neglected my children at times when I should have been there for them. I know I am not alone as a parent questioning my parenting skills and decisions. But I do know that I have gotten older and wiser and I now make more flexible decisions as an adult and as a parent. I think things through a bit more now, in how I deal with my children.

Being flexible to me means sticking to your core values but also being willing to allow others theirs. Being flexible is about accepting criticism and not being complacent. I know that my children will make mistakes along the way just as I did. As a father, I want to be there for my children to give them love, support and guidance like my parents gave to me. I want to encourage my children to get back up when they fall down. I know I have made many parenting mistakes, but I will try my best to do better from this point on. It's never too late to be a better parent . . . and my children deserve it.

Divorced

Sheree and I are now divorced due to irreconcilable differences. Our divorce was finalized in 2009.

Reaching Success

It probably was a big surprise to many of you to know that I was so insecure about my success. In fact it took me years to admit that fear was at the root of my performance. It goes against much of what the literature and "gurus" out there are insisting that you have to let go of your fear to ever become successful. The gurus also say that you cannot be afraid to fail. Actually, I don't think that's an absolute. My fear of failing as a child carried over onto the football field in high school, college and the

NFL. I was so concerned about not being successful that it pushed me to be successful.

All of those extra hours in the gym or the track or on the practice field, were more than just about hard work; it was about avoiding failure. Before every game of my NFL career I was afraid to fail, afraid that I would not be good enough, afraid that I would let my teammates down. I was very insecure about everything. But now, after all these years, I realized it all goes back to me not wanting to let my father down. I did not want to disappoint him. My dad always told me he wanted me to be better than he was and to go further in sports than he did. He wanted me to be a great player in the sport that I loved. He never wanted me to be just good - he wanted me to be great. And I always tried my best not to disappoint him.

Working hard is all I know. Working hard is about going that extra mile, taking a step away from safe shores to experience all that life has to offer. It took me many years to learn how to suck the marrow out of life and recognize what was driving me on the inside.

I found out later in life that drive was the key to my success and it could be for you as well. I hope that you enjoy my book as much as I did living it. But more importantly, I hope you are enjoying your own journey. Nothing lasts forever so enjoy what you have and don't turn back.

Robert Tate

Chapter 15

Hanging up the Cleats

When it came time to hang up the cleats, it was a tremendous adjustment for me. This transition was so great because I was healthy and my body was still in good shape and I felt like I still had at least two more good years in myself to play the game. Yes, I miss the routine of preparing to play on Sundays. Yes, I miss the fans shouting my name when I run out of the tunnel on game day. Yes, I miss the competitiveness of playing the game each week. So yes, it was very hard for me to walk away from the game that I love so much.

The transition from the NFL to civilian life is a very difficult transition for many athletes. I went through a serious changeover in my life when professional football was no longer a part of it. I think I even missed the structure that football provided. Football had been a part of my life since I was seven years old. So leaving the game was very emotional for me. I didn't know what I was going to do to fill the void that football left in my life. It was a very scary feeling and I went through some emotional changes in my life.

Now that I have come to terms with the fact that I am no longer playing football in the NFL, I have moved on with my life.

The ACES

For about a year, I worked for The ACES in Tempe, Arizona as a behavior coach. The ACES is a state certified special education private school for special needs students ranging in age from 5 to 21. I worked with the younger children. Some of my responsibilities as a behavior coach were to help motivate and encourage learning in the students' education. In that process, I used the strengths and interests of the kids to help motivate them. I worked hard to make assignments fun and engaging. It brought great joy to my heart to see the smiles, the relief and the self-confidence on their faces when a homework assignment was completed correctly or when a student completed a seemingly hard project. I enjoyed working with these children and using their strengths and interests to help empower them. I wanted them to be able to reach the next level and to overcome their next challenge; no matter what obstacle got in the way. My goal for the children I worked with was to help them to stay focused and reach their full potential. I also wanted to instill in them that with hard work and determination, they could be anything they wanted to be in life.

It was not about the money for me to work at the ACES, it was about me being able to give something back to these children who are struggling with learning disabilities. I felt that I was an effective behavior coach because I had already gone through what most of these children were going through with their learning disabilities and I understood their needs. Working for The ACES was therapeutic and very fulfilling for me in my transition from the NFL. I truly hope I was able to help make a difference in a young person's life at The ACES.

Moving On

I am now going to keep working hard at every new challenge in my life and seek out opportunities that I never thought possible.

I had a great career in the NFL, but now, at the end of my professional football career, as I look back over all my early struggles, what I had to overcome and how much I have accomplished in my life, I have to smile, give myself a pat on the back and say, "Job Well Done!"

Robert Tate

Chapter 16

Overcoming Dyslexia

For many years I hid behind my dyslexia because I was embarrassed about being dyslexic and I didn't want to have that label attached to my name. I didn't want my peers to think that something was wrong with me. I told my mom not to tell anyone about my condition, including family, because this was my battle and no one needed to know my struggles. So no one ever knew, not even the ones I was closest too.

After I attained success, my mom told me there is someone out there who needs to hear my story of determination and triumph and she insisted that I tell my story. She wanted me to reveal my struggles with my secret battle with dyslexia. After putting it off for many months, I finally wrote a book about my early struggles and it provided an enormous inner healing for me.

I now spread the word about overcoming obstacles by doing motivational speaker engagements and workshops in schools, churches and seminars about challenges our youth are faced with on a daily basis and what they need to do to overcome those challenges.

Robert Tate

I thank my mother, Michele, for insisting that I tell my story. It was a story that did need to be told. I just pray that my story touches someone in a mighty way so they will see that it is not the end of the world when you are faced with challenges or if obstacles get in the way.

I overcame my challenges and with a lot of hard work, goal setting, perseverance and dedication, you can overcome too.

To your success!

Afterword

It was a great experience to work in the NFL, but I want our youth to know that football and basketball is not everything. Education comes first. I know we all want to be the next Michael Jordan in basketball or the next Johnny Unitas in football. But you can't let the sport be your only dream; you must have a back-up plan. You have to realize that there are many great players who never make it to the elite NFL or NBA, no matter how good they are.

Our youth also need role models they can touch, not like Kobe Bryant, Shaquille O'Neill, Donovan McNabb or Peyton Manning who most of them will never see. I'm not ashamed to say that my role model is my mother and its okay. My mother is an amazing lady of strength and character and I love and respect her.

I want to instill in our youth that there is so much more they can offer other than making a dunk or a touchdown. I want to instill upon our youth the importance of working hard in school along with playing sports because at the end of the day, there is no guarantee that they will be able to ever play professional sports. However, getting an education will open the door of opportunity for them to be anything they want to be in life.

Robert Tate

Do not let any obstacle or challenge in your life stop you from achieving your dream.

In Closing Regarding Dyslexia

Over the years, in my research of dyslexia, I have discovered that there are millions of school children with dyslexia. These children endure a lot of pain and suffering because of this learning disability. On a daily basis, they go through all kinds of emotions in school such as: dejection, frustration, sadness, despair and hopelessness. Some children even end up having to deal with depression as well. They struggle to acquire skills that many of their classmates take for granted such as the basic reading and writing skills. Many parents don't know that help is available for their children who suffer from dyslexia.

I am very familiar of the struggle with dyslexia because I have dyslexia and I went through all the emotions that I mentioned above. There was not a lot of help in the schools for children with dyslexia back then and my mom could only find limited resources that were available. However, thankfully, she did discover Sylvan Learning Center and she enrolled me in their tutoring program. It made all the difference in the world for me. I got my self-confidence back and my transformation in the classroom was nothing short of amazing.

Unlike when I was in elementary school, help is now readily available for children with dyslexia and I am going to do my part to spread the word to parents that help is obtainable for your dyslexic child.

Today there are many Children's Learning Centers for Dyslexia and they are readily available to assist children and their families to overcome the painful obstacles of dyslexia.

I fully and whole-heartedly stand behind the Sylvan Learning Center being the difference between success and failure for children with dyslexia. I believe in them so much that I have added Sylvan Learning Center to my Robert Tate Foundation www.roberttatenow.com to raise money for all the good work that they do for our young children with dyslexia. My wish is that any child with dyslexia will have the opportunity to receive tutoring by trained personnel at a Children's Learning Center nationwide.

Our children are our future and we need to give them love, support, encouragement and the tools they need to succeed. Sylvan Learning Center can help children and their families overcome the painful obstacles of dyslexia so they can enjoy a successful happy life.

With the help and guidance of highly skilled and dedicated tutors at a Children's Learning Center for dyslexia, our children can reach success that they never thought possible!

NFL Teams

Apr.   1997-2002: Drafted by the Minnesota Vikings in the 6th round.

Aug.   2002-2003: Signed as an unrestricted free agent by the Baltimore Ravens.

Jan.   2003-2004: Did not play football this season

Feb.   2004-2007: Signed as a free agent by the Arizona Cardinals.

College Accomplishments

1994 Prep Team Offensive Player of the Week

1994 Special Teams Player of the Year

1995 Named C-USA Offensive Player of the Week

1995 AT&T Long Distance Award

1996 National Kickoff Return Title

1996 The Claude Rost Most Valuable Player Award

1997 Played in the Senior Bowl in Mobile, Alabama

High School Accomplishments

1990-92 All American High School Running Back

1991 YMCA of Greater Harrisburg Youth of the Year

1991 High School State Champs 4x100 (anchor)

1990-91 Undefeated MPC Champs

1991 Keystone State Games Championship Team

1992 McDonald's High School Basketball Team selection

1992 Big 33 Football Classic selection

1992-93 Patriot News "Big 15"

Robert Tate

mom and me

174

Another Book

If you enjoyed reading this book about determination and triumph, you will absolutely love reading his mother's book. The book is titled:

Breaking All Barriers

How A Teen Mom Took Her Son From Dyslexia to the NFL

By Michele Burnett Tate Washington

$17.95

You can order this book online at
www.breakingallbarriers.com

Robert Tate

About the Author

Robert Tate was drafted as a wide receiver but made the switch to defensive back midway through the 1999 season, and later became only the second player in Vikings history to record a pass reception and pass interception in the same season.

Tate was a veteran of nine NFL seasons. He spent five years with Head Coach Dennis Green with the Minnesota Vikings. After being released from the Vikings in 2002, Tate played one year for the Baltimore Ravens with Head Coach Brian Billick. After his one year stint in Baltimore, Tate was reunited with Head Coach Dennis Green and played three years for the Arizona Cardinals.

Although Tate is no longer in the NFL, he continues to remain busy as an author, a motivational speaker and trainer encouraging youth not to give up on their dreams. He helps youth find the keys to personal potential and fulfillment through his speaking engagements.

Robert Tate

Book Robert Tate for your next event. He does speaking engagements at seminars, schools, churches and athletic events. Tate's speeches are highly inspirational. Be prepared for all listeners to be ignited by Tate's fiery passion in his keynote speeches.

Robert's Theme Message is Focus

Follow

On

Course

Until

Successful

Robert Tate's website: www.roberttatenow.com

You can also contact Robert Tate at:

(612) 306-8668 **or** (717) 623-7698

Robert Tate

Quick Order Form

These books are also available at a discount for bulk purchases for educational use. For special pricing, call Robert Tate at (612) 306-8668.

Telephone Orders: Call (717) 623-7698 or (612) 306-8668 – Have your credit card ready.

Email Orders: roberttatenow@yahoo.com

Order On-line: www.roberttatenow.com

Mail Orders:
Robert Tate Now
P. O. Box 61904
Harrisburg, PA 17106

Make checks payable to Robert Tate
Your Name _____
Your Address _____

_____

Book Title: Robert Tate-From Little League to the NFL

Cost: $19.95 + $2.50 Shipping and Handling

Total Cost: $22.45

Made in the USA
Lexington, KY
22 March 2015